Critical Encounters with Immersive Storytelling

A uniquely interdisciplinary look at storytelling in digital, analogue, and hybridised contexts, this book traces different ways stories are experienced in our contemporary mediascape. It uses an engaging range of current examples to explore interactive and immersive narratives.

Critical Encounters with Immersive Storytelling considers exciting new forms of storytelling that are emerging in contemporary popular culture. Here, immersion is being facilitated in a variety of ways and in a multitude of contexts, from 3D cinema to street games, from immersive theatre plays to built environments such as theme parks, as well as in a multitude of digital formats. The book explores diverse modes and practices of immersive storytelling, discussing what is gained and lost in each of these 'genres'. Building on notions of experience and immersion, it suggests a framework within which we might begin to understand the quality of being immersed. It also explores the practical and ethical aspects of this exciting and evolving terrain.

This accessible and lively study will be of great interest to students and researchers of media studies, digital culture, games studies, extended reality, experience design, and storytelling.

Dr. Alke Gröppel-Wegener is an Associate Professor of Creative Academic Practice at Staffordshire University where she teaches as part of the animation team. She is interested in the retelling and regenreing of stories in all forms. As a National Teaching Fellow, she retells 'hidden' academic practice in visual metaphors (some collected in *Writing Essays by Pictures*, Innovative Libraries 2016), blogging about her work at www.tactileacademia.com. Her research focuses on the design of experiences, in particular within theme parks.

Dr. Jenny Kidd is a Senior Lecturer in the School of Journalism, Media and Culture at Cardiff University. Jenny researches across the fields of digital media and digital cultural heritage studies, often in collaboration with partners in the cultural sector. She is the author of *Museums in the New Mediascape: Transmedia, Participation, Ethics* (Routledge 2014) and *Representation* (Routledge 2015). She has published widely on participatory media, transmedia, and immersive heritage. Jenny has been a core project partner on a number of immersive storytelling projects, including *With New Eyes I See* (2014) and *Traces/Olion* (2016). www.jennykidd.org

Critical Encounters with Immersive Storytelling

Alke Gröppel-Wegener
and Jenny Kidd

NEW YORK AND LONDON

First published 2019
by Routledge
52 Vanderbilt Avenue, New York, NY 10017

and by Routledge
2 Park Square, Milton Park, Abingdon, Oxon, OX14 4RN

Routledge is an imprint of the Taylor & Francis Group, an informa business

First issued in paperback 2021

© 2019 Taylor & Francis

The right of Alke Gröppel-Wegener and Jenny Kidd to be identified as authors of this work has been asserted by them in accordance with sections 77 and 78 of the Copyright, Designs and Patents Act 1988.

All rights reserved. No part of this book may be reprinted or reproduced or utilised in any form or by any electronic, mechanical, or other means, now known or hereafter invented, including photocopying and recording, or in any information storage or retrieval system, without permission in writing from the publishers.

Trademark notice: Product or corporate names may be trademarks or registered trademarks, and are used only for identification and explanation without intent to infringe.

Library of Congress Cataloging-in-Publication Data
A catalog record for this title has been requested

ISBN: 978-0-367-15162-1 (hbk)
ISBN: 978-1-03-209395-6 (pbk)
ISBN: 978-0-429-05540-9 (ebk)

Typeset in Times New Roman
by codeMantra

Contents

	List of Figures	vi
1	Introduction: The Seductive Power of Immersion	1
2	Layers of Experience	21
3	*Traces*: A Case Study	60
4	Against Immersion?	85
5	Conclusion	104
	Bibliography	107
	Glossary of Examples	117
	Index	133

Figures

1.1 'The Big Blue Pool' at the Art of Animation Resort hotel at Walt Disney World (Credit: Alke Gröppel-Wegener)   4
1.2 Martina Amati 'Under'. Installation view in *Somewhere in Between* at Wellcome Collection, 2018 (Credit: Wellcome Collection)   6
1.3 *Rain Room* is an artwork where the visitor is immersed in a downpour, but due to the use of motion detectors does not get wet (Credit: RANDOM INTERNATIONAL, Rain Room, 2012. Exhibited at The Curve, Barbican, London. Courtesy of The Maxine and Stuart Frankel Foundation for Art)   12
1.4 Seals at the 'North Pole Encounter', part of *Polar Adventure* at Ocean Park (Credit: Alke Gröppel-Wegener)   16
2.1 Layers of Experience overview   28
2.2 Map of *Harry Potter: A History of Magic* exhibition at the British Library (Credit: British Library)   41
2.3 *The Wizarding World of Harry Potter – Diagon Alley* themed land at Universal Studios Florida (Credit: Alke Gröppel-Wegener)   44
2.4 *The Wizarding World of Harry Potter – Hogsmeade* at Universal Islands of Adventure (Credit: Alke Gröppel-Wegener)   57
3.1 *Traces/Olion* logo (Credit: Hoffi/yello brick)   61
3.2 Alke's field notes from her *Traces* experience (Credit: Alke Gröppel-Wegener)   62
3.3 Becoming immersed in a tunnel made of trees while exploring *Traces* (Credit: Jenny Kidd)   64

3.4	Sketches used in the *Traces* app (Credit: Hoffi/yello brick)	69
3.5	Screen grabs from the *Traces* app (Credit: Hoffi/yello brick)	71
3.6	Sample participant mapping of *Traces* (Credit: image from project evaluation)	73
3.7	On the partner experience of *Olion,* the Welsh language equivalent of *Traces* (Credit: Alison John)	78

1 Introduction

The Seductive Power of Immersion

Doing 'something immersive' is increasingly seen as a way of maintaining relevance and securing visibility in a crowded and complex content landscape. As this book will demonstrate, the quality of *being immersed* is facilitated in diverse ways and in a multitude of contexts. While the term has more recently been used to describe developments in the fields of Virtual Reality (VR), Augmented Reality (AR), and mixed reality, there are many analogue experiences that can be considered immersive: street games, interactive theatre, and built environments such as theme parks and historic sites, for example. Indeed, many forms of immersive storytelling collapse the binary between physical and digital contexts, allowing holistic storyworlds to be constructed and inhabited. Immersive storytelling is exciting and evolving terrain, raising practical and ethical questions as we investigate here.

This book uses a range of current examples to explore different forms of storytelling. It understands much compelling and creative contemporary story-making to be collaborative, transmedial, multimodal, experiential, performative, and (sometimes) ungovernable. Focusing on diverse practices, the book traces different ways stories are being experienced in our contemporary mediascape, discussing what is gained and lost in different genres of immersive storytelling. It unpacks complex terms to suggest a framework within which we begin to understand the quality and promise of immersion. We critically analyse the 'immersive turn' within its broadest creative, cultural, technological, and social contexts, whilst recognising it as an increasingly economic and political project as well. Examples are drawn internationally, reflecting the fact that immersive media are the subject of transnational popular and scholarly attention.

We (the authors) have both been researching at the intersection of immersion and storytelling for many years, exploring diverse connections between narrative, genre, environments, and experience.

2 Introduction

Our joint perspective makes this book a unique resource; it is both critically and practically attuned, and offers ways into research design for immersive contexts. Such research raises complex methodological considerations that are often rendered invisible in the reporting of case studies; yet, this book acknowledges and confronts them head on, making our reflexivity visible, and itself a productive resource.

This introductory chapter considers some key themes, concepts, and approaches that we return to throughout the book. It uses existing scholarship to explore what we mean when we talk about 'immersion' and 'storytelling', noting that neither concept is bounded or stable. It examines why 'the immersive' is such a seductive concept in our present cultural, social, economic, and political moment(s), and thus why its study is important. It introduces key concepts that will underpin analyses in the book and begins to problematise meaningful distinctions between analogue/digital, physical/virtual, and online/offline.

Given the complexity of immersive storytelling as a research subject, we now offer four different approaches to sketch out where this book sits – the analogy, the experience, the history, and the definition – before concluding with an overview of the book's structure.

The Analogy: Liquid Metaphors and the Glass-Bottomed Boat

We as researchers come to this writing project from not quite opposite, but certainly different, directions and perspectives. Alke's background is in theatre design and she has had a fascination with how theme parks work ever since having to write a paper on English Garden Architecture as an undergraduate student. Subsequently, she investigated what museums can learn from theme park design, and became interested in how story experiences can be created without performers. Jenny's background as a web developer and (then) digital storytelling researcher later led her to research within cultural heritage contexts, with a particular interest in their performative and digital dimensions. In recent years, that has included action research in the build, test, and evaluation stages of immersive projects. We met more than a decade ago at an event put on by a museum theatre company we were both working with at the time, albeit on different projects. This event had on the surface all the hallmarks of an immersive experience: a themed environment, a (fictional) backstory, and performers that were interacting with the audience as characters. But neither of us felt fully immersed, and at times the experience was downright uncomfortable. We have had many conversations since that time, attempting to understand what was happening.

Consulting scholarship has helped us little in our reflections on this immersive encounter: According to Matthew Reason, the term 'immersive' is one with 'extremely tricky conceptual grounding' (2015: 272). Alison McMahon proposed in 2003 that the concept of immersion in video games had become 'an excessively vague, all-inclusive concept' (2003: 67) and Adam Alston has more recently observed that 'the immersive label is flexible' to the degree that it can 'jeapordize terminological clarity' (2013: 128). No clear definition exists; yet, we all seem to have an idea of what we are talking about when we use that word 'immersive'.

Maybe it is most helpful to consider, as many have done before (see Machon 2013; Lukas 2016, for example), the analogy of water to introduce the idea of immersion. This is an idea we explore in this section, as well as in the images that accompany this chapter demonstrating different practices and levels of immersion. 'Liquid metaphors' (Wolf 2012: 49) are tantalising because they emerge etymologically from the word 'immersion' itself, and they indicate that there might be different levels or degrees here to 'get wet': we could throw a water balloon onto, or empty a bucket of water over, somebody, 'immersing' them for a split second; that person could stand in a waterfall, which might mean a longer and more intensive experience; we could partly immerse somebody, like in a bathtub; or we could go into a full diving mode, sending somebody to the depths of the sea – deep immersion. In the context of crafting theme park experiences, David Younger explains how designer Tim Kirk thinks about guests as 'Waders', 'Swimmers', and 'Divers' – and designs experiences to allow them to choose their own level of immersion:

> The Waders just want to walk around and see pretty pictures. The Swimmers want to get a little deeper; they might want some backstory, they might want to get into it a little more. And the Divers really want to know every shred of information that exists about that particular subject. We give them all this backstory in case they're really, really interested, and if not that's okay – they don't have to read it, or they don't have to look at it, and for the most part they don't really do. At one level, they just want to ride the ride.
>
> (Kirk in Younger 2016: 84)

4 *Introduction*

All of these stages of 'liquid immersion' have their equivalents in immersive storytelling and we will draw on some of them as examples. However, what we are really interested in is deep immersion, perhaps the most difficult to achieve and the trickiest to analyse.

The event we met at cast both of us not as being immersed ourselves, but rather as sitting in a glass-bottomed boat watching other people being immersed. Occasionally we would get splashed by water. Overall it was a bit weird. The event and our experiences of it raised searching questions about immersive storytelling as 'form', and about the limits of our methodologies for beginning to unpack it. This was in hindsight our initiation into the fragile and intriguing

Figure 1.1 'The Big Blue Pool' at the Art of Animation Resort hotel at Walt Disney World is themed after the film *Finding Nemo*, ideal for 'waders' and 'swimmers' (in the liquid immersion sense): You can just splash about enjoying a nicely designed environment, you can connect with a story you already know, or you can become part of the story while playing (Credit: Alke Gröppel-Wegener).

world of immersive experiences, an initiation that oriented us towards the pursuit of more – and better – opportunities for immersion. Over the years we discussed this issue, as well as going on trips to check out immersive experiences around the UK. At a catch-up meeting in late 2017, we discussed our current projects, our teaching, and how much our own processes had developed since our first meeting. We concluded that there wasn't really a book out there that provided an accessible introduction to immersive storytelling contexts and how to approach researching them (by now 'immersive' was quite a buzzword and probably overused). Having wanted to do a project together for about a decade, we decided to write it ourselves.

The Experience: Story as an Agent of Immersion

Unfortunately the water analogy only gets us so far. As analogies are likely to do, it provides a model of one aspect of immersion and ignores others. Using the liquid metaphor might mean that we pay too much attention to what surrounds an individual (or individuals) having the experience, as if an experience was external, which of course it isn't. An experience, in the way we are understanding it here, is at the end of the day an internal and subjective phenomenon. Therefore, we also need to somewhat unpick the complex notion of 'experience' (Lash 2006) if we want to make headway in the area of immersive storytelling.

Many immersive experiences privilege multi-sensorial encounters. As Josephine Machon notes 'in immersive practice, because all of one's senses are heightened, it is difficult not to become acutely aware of the natural aromas of the space, of polished wood floorboards, of dank cellars, of earthy green woods' (Machon 2013: 76). Such sensory stimulation brings participants into an immediate and felt entanglement with the practice, whether positively or negatively experienced. A number of researchers have activated multimodality as a framework through which to explore immersive work (Kenderdine 2016; Kidd 2017; Galani and Kidd 2019), an approach that makes perfect sense when thinking about examples that literally surround you, like immersive theatre, theme parks, or a 360 degree art installation such as Martina Amati's **'Under'** (see Figure 1.2).[1]

But can this also apply to our analysis of something seemingly as simple as the experience of reading a book? People often talk about 'being immersed' in a book, and the idea of losing yourself

6 *Introduction*

Figure 1.2 Martina Amati 'Under'. Installation view in *Somewhere in Between* at Wellcome Collection, 2018. Here, visitors find themselves in an exhibition space surrounded by large-scale video projections of freedivers in ethereal and intricate under-water performances (Credit: Wellcome Collection).

in a fantasy world and going on adventures with the characters you encounter there is certainly a very seductive one. Thinking about the actual medium of words on a page, it seems unlikely that books can provide immersive storytelling experiences in the manner described above, after all there is nothing to tie up the senses beyond the visual, no inclusion of taste or smell (beyond the smell of the book itself, which is probably not connected to the content of any story within), and even sight can be easily distracted in most situations you are likely to read a book.

Yet, the idea of the immersive book (or story) is one that has fascinated storytellers for quite some time. *The Neverending Story* by Michael Ende,[2] for example, tells of a boy who slowly becomes immersed in a book. The first half of the novel is about him first acquiring and then reading the book. It describes how he becomes immersed, not only in his reading (we read what he reads, but also what he thinks about what he is reading), but through his interactions with the characters. In time – and in the middle of the book the reader is reading – the boy enters the book (or story), becoming immersed in it in the most comprehensive way, by becoming a character in its narrative. The idea of entering a fictitious world is not that uncommon in both literature and film. Jasper Fforde's *Thursday Next* book series, for example, portrays a protagonist who can bookjump, 'read' herself into books and interact with the characters in them (most of them aware that they are fictitious characters). It also happens in films, for example in *The Purple Rose of Cairo* (1985), a film character comes into the real world from the silver screen and later takes a character from the real world into his world. In *The Last Action Hero* (1993), a child is given the opportunity to enter a movie and later needs to take its action hero back with him into the real world in order to track down the villain who has also escaped. In the TV series *Lost in Austen* (2008), a woman discovers a portal into *Pride and Prejudice* and ends up swapping places with the heroine and changing the narrative.

Yet, *The Neverending Story* (in at least some of its editions), goes a step further and cleverly ties the reader into the protagonist's adventures by being presented as itself the book the boy is reading. When the copper-coloured cover featuring embossed snakes is described, it is difficult not to partially close the book to check the book you are holding, which is exactly as described within. When it is mentioned that there are two different colours of type within the book he holds, you realise that you have spotted the same two different colours of type within the book in your hand. Could you really be reading the same book that he is? Linking the content of the reading experience with its mode of presentation makes *The Neverending Story* one example where immersion is employed in a slightly different way – by making use of the real world as a touchstone that actually emphasises the experience you are having, and making the fantasy more real at the same time.[3]

The promise of becoming part of a story by either re-living a familiar scene or taking a protagonist's place and changing the narrative is evidently a seductive one. Whole new genres of story-making have developed around that possibility such as CosPlay and Live Action Role Playing (LARPing).

Reading a book is about more than just reading a text then. Mangen (2008) references the multi-sensorial nature of all reading, although noting that it is a neglected area of research. 'Haptic perception' she notes 'is of vital importance to reading, and should be duly acknowledged'. 'Materiality matters' she concludes (Mangen 2008: 405). However, analyses of these dimensions are complex given that, as Linda Candy states, 'every human being senses the world with perceptual faculties common to us all and yet each individual differs in the exact nature of that experience' (2014: 36). This is an important reminder that processes of participation, immersion, and interaction are not straightforward, a point we will revisit again and again in this book.

So whilst the materiality of *how* an immersive experience is delivered matters – be it virtual or analogue – storytelling experiences have other dimensions that we explore in this book. This is the reason why, as the title of the book suggests, story is one of the central themes we explore.

The History: Story, Interaction, and Immersion

This section traces a (necessarily brief) history of the ways storytelling, interaction, and immersion intersect. It will be seen that interaction and immersion have been central to peoples' experiences of story through time (Ong 1982; Toolan 1988; Herman 2002). Technology has been enmeshed with these developments (although not a sole driver of them), so this section is also one that centres and is informed by media history.

The storying of events has long been understood as crucial to the development and maintenance of life and our understanding of our place or meaning within it. As Yilmaz and Ciğerci assert, 'the history of storytelling is as old as human history' (2018: 2). Much has been written about the ways our cultures and histories are 'storied', noting that storytellers themselves have tended to have a great amount of power and influence within their communities. As Howard E. Gardner notes, 'stories, including narratives, myths, and fables, constitute a uniquely powerful currency in human relationships' (1995: 42). Stories are also crucial to the creation of identity and a notion of 'self' (McAdams 1993); according to Finnegan, the self is 'formulated and experienced through self-narratives' (Finnegan 1997: 69). We now experience stories endlessly, in our leisure time, through work, our politics, our education, and through increasingly personalised, narrativised, and responsive advertising campaigns. Stories in the media help shape our societies and inform our agendas (although not simplistically as media and communications scholarship continues to remind us). Stories proliferate.

During the nineteenth century, technological developments such as the telegraph and later the telephone led to new ways of communicating across time and space (McLuhan 1964: 97). These technologies would form the basis of an explosion of media and narrative that would involve radio, cinema, and eventually television – Ong's 'secondary orality' (Ong 1982: 133). Since the advent of computing and digital media, many different pathways into – and through – narrative have emerged, not least computer games, VR, social media, data visualisation, and online streaming. YouTube, for example, has been a site of incredible dynamism within this space, impacting practices of audiencing, but more significantly perhaps content production and the business models that underpin it (Burgess and Green 2018). The World Wide Web is full of new and exciting ways of constructing, accessing, and monetising narrative (McErlean 2018), self-publishing, hypertext storytelling, the playing of character games such as *World of Warcraft* online, and the submission of stories to news websites, for example. Ruth E. Page writes compellingly about multiple different forms of storytelling via social media including in Wikipedia, Facebook updates, and the Twittersphere (2012, 2018). The web has become a live site for stories to be written and shared with a (possibly) global audience. It might be posited that 'the ancient art of storytelling is not lost but reformed' (Sloane 2000: 7) in storytelling mechanisms that are native to the internet and digital logics (Rose 2011).

In the book publishing industry, these shifts were preceded by a number of other developments that saw narrative beginning to push at the boundaries of the page. 'Choose your own ending' children's books first appeared in the late 1970s (for example Packard and Montgomery's *Choose Your Own Adventure* books launched in 1979), and a number of high-profile publications that ignored or questioned the conventions of linear narrative, Alasdair Gray's *Lanark* (1981) and B.S. Johnson's *The Unfortunates* (1969) for example. The latter was published as a box containing unbound sections to be read in any order, an attempt to liberate the book from the tyranny of the spine. Janet Murray noted in 1997 that 'twentieth-century novels, films, and plays have been steadily pushing against the boundaries of linear storytelling' (Murray 1997: 29), and we have seen this experimentation continue, and proliferate, into the twenty-first century as well (Ryan 2004; Ryan and Thon 2014). More recently, the Doug Dorst and J.J. Abrams story *S* (2013) is presented in a conversation of handwritten notes within a fictional library book, leaving the reader a multitude of ways to encounter the narrative. The work of the Visual Editions publishing team on the Editions at Play series (with Google Creative Labs Sydney) is quite remarkable in this space, including, for example, Kate Pullinger's **Breathe** (2018)[4] which accesses data via your mobile phone in order to 'internalise the world around you' as you read (Pullinger 2018).

10 *Introduction*

We note elsewhere in this book that our approach to immersive storytelling takes us beyond an elision with VR or AR, but it is important to introduce these developments here also. VR – a term introduced by Jaron Lanier in the 1980s – tends to refer to a very particular set of practices. For Frederick Brooks, there are three key features: real-time rendering and viewpoint changes (as a participant moves their head), a virtual environment (concrete or abstract), and interaction (in Steinicke 2016: viii). VR is perhaps most recognisable in the form of interaction through head-mounted displays, but it has had a long and difficult coming of age, as yet failing to live up to its promise, in part (according to John Bucher) because audiences continue to seek out 'linear logic' for storytelling rather than experiences (like VR) where 'chronology and causality tak[e] lesser roles' (2017: 84). AR experiences differ in that they offer a composite view of both the 'real world' and a layer of digital content superimposed on top. AR applications such as Snapchat (launched 2011) and numerous experiential advertising campaigns have introduced many more people to the possibilities of digital media for world building and blended experiences. Examples of the latter include a 2015 AR campaign for VISA that featured interactive digital content (such as 'life size' giraffes, elephants, and pandas) layered onto the real-world environment of a shopping centre in Poland, and the 2017 launch of the IKEA Place app that enabled users to see what products would look like within their own home. Industry professionals have begun to talk across this range of activities as Extended Reality (XR).

It is in this context – and including the VR precursor of the video game in all its forms – that a large chunk of scholarship on immersion is located. Here, immersion is principally understood as the extent to which 'computer displays are capable of delivering an inclusive, extensive, surrounding and vivid illusion of the reality to the senses of a human participant.' (Slater and Wilbur 1997: 3) 'Presence', that is, 'the (psychological) sense of being in [a] virtual environment' (Slater and Wilbur 1997: 4), has been a particularly influential concept within that scholarship, leading to the pursuit of ever more sophisticated virtual environments so that participants might 'consider the environment specified by the displays as places visited rather than as images seen.' (Slater and Wilbur 1997: 4) Our use of the term immersion incorporates – but does not depend on – this notion of presence, given that we wish to work across a more comprehensive set of experiences.

Introduction 11

Other concepts considered within video games scholarship that contribute to both immersion and presence are the notions of flow (Csikszentmihalyi 1990) and engagement.[5] Seah and Cairns argue that immersion is different, but related, to flow.

> Flow is a harmonious psychological state whereby a person is engaged in an activity that is challenging but not beyond the skills of the person and has a clear sense of progression towards a goal. The outcome is a positive and rewarding experience.
> (Seah and Cairns 2008: 2)

They go on to argue that games can be immersive without providing flow and hypothesise that 'immersion is a precursor to flow. During flow, people are wholly engaged in their activity to the exclusion of all other concerns. This sense of being "lost to the world" matches well with the colloquial sense of immersion.' (Seah and Cairns 2008: 2)

In other developments, there has been increasing excitement about the possibilities of integrating our biomechanical information with immersive storytelling experiences (in for example *Jekyll 2.0*, Mandal 2015), as well as storytelling using artificial intelligence (see for example *It's No Game*, 2017), immersive documentaries (see the work of the **i-Docs** project), immersive journalism (such as *River of Mud*, 2016), immersive music (LA Philarmonic's *VAN Beethoven* VR application, 2015), immersive art applications (such as *Tiltbrush*) and immersive installations (such as the work of Random International on *Rain Room*, Figure 1.3). Immersive media have found their uses for military purposes also, including as training and recruitment tools (such as the US Marines' **Augmented Immersive Team Trainer**, 2016).

As the above demonstrates, and whilst anxious not to overplay the role of the digital in processes of immersion (ours is not a 'technocratic' approach[6]), there are interesting things happening at the boundaries of the digital and the physical (Petrelli et al. 2013). 'Hybrid' (Causey 2016; Ciolfi 2017) and 'mixed reality' (Ohta and Tamura 1999) experiences are becoming more common, and it is increasingly recognised that the distinction between being online and being offline needs to be problematised. Kevin Moloney's term 'postdigital narrative' is perhaps a helpful one in this regard (2012). Today's uses of digital media are not disembodied, as recognised in investigations into haptic technologies for example, and Anne Mangen has proposed that researchers should pay more attention

12 *Introduction*

Figure 1.3 *Rain Room* is an artwork where the visitor is immersed in a downpour, but due to the use of motion detectors does not get wet (Credit: RANDOM INTERNATIONAL, Rain Room, 2012. Exhibited at The Curve, Barbican, London. Courtesy of The Maxine and Stuart Frankel Foundation for Art).

to the role our bodies, and in particular our fingers and hands, play in what she terms 'immersive fiction reading' experiences via digital devices (2008). Although we downplay the centrality of digital media in definitional terms in this book, much immersive storytelling practice does demonstrate and benefit from what might be termed 'thinking digitally' (Causey 2016: 436).

In recent years, and as allied to the experimentation with VR, AR, and XR above, there has been much focus on the spatial components of immersive storytelling. Jason Farman (2014b, 2015) reminds us that these are not new concerns however, noting links between story and space through time: 'Storytelling is important for the production and practice of space because the meaning of a space is typically communicated through the stories attached to those spaces ... stories, spaces, and communities are intimately tied together' (Farman 2015: 101). The possibilities presented by spatial immersion in storyworlds have been explored in theme parks for quite some time, but have perhaps been most epically demonstrated in recent years in the popularity of the ***Pokémon Go*** mobile application. There have been many other explorations at the intersections of story, space, and immersion; in studies of cultural heritage, for example, there have been many attempts to play at the interstices of space and story, often facilitated via digital technologies (Keil et al. 2013; Ciolfi and McLoughlin 2017; Kidd 2017; Poole 2017). Historic Royal Palaces' *The Lost Palace* (2016) has attempted to 're-create' the lost Palace of Whitehall in its original location (it burned down in 1698) using haptic technologies and binaural (3D spatial audio) sound, and Alberto Galindo demonstrates how a mobile application can be used to connect people with stories in space in his overview of the making of the 9/11 Memorial Museum mobile application (2014).

Texts on spatialised narrative (Rieser 2005; Ryan et al. 2016; Kitchin et al. 2017), locative narrative (Ritchie 2014), mobile art (Rieser 2011), and increased focus on storytelling media as 'pervasive' and 'ambient' (Ambient Literature 2016) indicate the depth of possibilities for thinking about story and space. As Rob Kitchin, Tracey P. Lauriault, and Matthew W. Wilson argue, geography is becoming a key 'organizational logic' on the web (2017: 2), but we might say beyond that also when it comes to experimentation with story and experience. For example, Anežka Kuzmičová, Theresa Schilhab, and Michael Burke note in their study of fiction reading on mobile phones (m-reading) that 'immediate environment and broader situational context' give reading via mobile 'unique affordances' (2018: 1). Story becomes enmeshed with, and informed by, its environment. In this book, we look at a variety of ways stories and storyworlds intersect with space, and consider how immersive interaction can alter our sense of a particular place, and our future encounters with it. This is most vividly demonstrated in Chapter 3 where we look at the *Traces/Olion* project, an immersive site-specific storytelling encounter at St Fagans National Museum of History, Wales.

We also note more nuanced treatment of the term 'participation' emerging in scholarship, and respond to it in this book. Jason Warren observes that even though five practitioners might offer 'five different answers' if asked to define immersive theatre, they would all agree that 'it's a form that gives the audience greater access to the performance ... to become part of the artistry rather than just spectators' (Warren 2017: vii). John Bucher notes in his study of VR contexts that 'storytelling ... is less about telling the viewer a story and more about letting the viewer discover the story' (Bucher 2017: 7). In scholarship about art, theatre, human computer interaction, and games, 'the term audience becomes vexed' (Machon 2013: 92) and the term 'participant' dominates (in Candy and Ferguson 2014 for example). Interactions within immersive storyworlds can be 'planned or unplanned' (White 2012: 230), and some might be facilitated through more extensive framing than others; an actual or metaphorical 'contract' between maker and participant. Some are built around threshold moments that are invaluable as markers for participation and immersion; Punchdrunk's **Small Wonders** (2018) for example uses a number of doorways to step immersion within the storyworld, and **Traces** (2016, outlined in detail in Chapter 3) uses a series of archways. This practice can also be found in literature, where Alice goes down the rabbit hole and Narnia can be accessed through the back of a wardrobe. Related is the theatre concept of the fourth wall – the imagined wall that completes the proscenium arch in a traditional theatre, which in some practices is 'broken' when performers directly address the audience (as also sometimes happens in filmic media). Suffice it to say that processes of participation are not straightforward, especially as responses to them have affective and evaluative dimensions that might be unique to individuals (Reason 2015).

It should be noted that while a traditional 'value chain' exists for many practices of cultural consumption (Paterson 2002), where a linear design – production – distribution process operates beyond (and precedes) often quite passive acts of consumption, many contemporary formats now disrupt that model. Sven Birkerts proposed that the advent of digital media would lead to traditional value chains being 'bent into a pretzel' (1994), and this we have begun to see, not least in the context of video sharing sites like YouTube, or crowdfunding platforms like Kickstarter.

There is thus a rich scholarship informing the individual themes covered in this book. But, as noted previously, there is no one text that responds to these developments by offering a framework for critically unpacking practice at the interstices of immersion and story. In the next section, we offer a definition of those practices, and in the next chapter, we go on to introduce that framework.

The Definition: Defining Immersive Storytelling for Our Purpose

We take a fairly broad understanding of immersion within the contexts of media and culture. This understanding is informed by our readings from a variety of subject areas not least immersive theatre, games, theme parks, human computer interaction, and studies of digital culture. Other scholars might set their boundaries around this term in different ways, but do tend to activate a similar lexical repertoire for talking about a set of features that are understood to characterise immersion. The coming together of these characteristics is variously described, but typically involves a collocation of perspectives on participation, space, the senses, and story. In her study of *Immersive Theatres*, Machon demonstrates that collocation of terms as she identifies the central features of immersive practice in informing her own definition: 'Audience involvement' (and 'audience evolvement'), 'a prioritization of the sensual world', and a recognition of 'the significance of space and place' (Machon 2013: 70). Nandita Dinesh's definition of immersive theatre similarly echoes these themes as she talks about 'a form that creates a multi-sensorial, participatory aesthetic for its spectators' (2016: 2), and Alston writes about 'theatre that surrounds audiences within an aesthetic space in which they are frequently, but not always, free to move and/or participate' (2013: 128). In talking about theme parks, Scott A. Lukas refers to immersion as 'the idea that a space and its multiple architectural, material, performative, and technological approaches may wrap up or envelop a guest within it' (2016: 3), and Alison Griffiths uses the term immersion to describe 'the sensation of entering a space that immediately identifies itself as somehow separate from the world and that eschews conventional modes of spectatorship in favor of more bodily participation in the experience' (2008: 2).

Our definition of immersive storytelling incorporates two tiers of practice explored in the chapters that follow. Firstly, we are interested in bounded encounters with story designed with deep immersion of groups or individuals in mind. Examples of this kind of practice include works of immersive theatre, street games, and VR experiences. These are (often) most easily understood as stand-alone encounters. Secondly, we are interested in the possibilities for immersion that come about when a number of different experiences are layered into more extensive and expansive 'storyworlds' (Harvey et al. 2014). Such storyworlds are often co-created by a multitude of creators and/or producers, ranging from brand and franchise storytellers to fans. These storyworlds can be transmediated, transnational, multilingual, and diachronically complex objects of study, and interacting with them often means being involved in a multilayered, multifaceted, and incredibly active unfurling of story ('official' and 'unofficial').

In the first kind of practice, the demarcation and isolation of 'an immersive activity' as an object of study is perhaps more

Figure 1.4 Via an underwater viewing window, the seals at the 'North Pole Encounter', part of *Polar Adventure* at Ocean Park, can be seen when they are fully immersed. While visitors are not immersed themselves, there is the opportunity to interact with the seals as part of a "Get Closer To The Animals" programmes (Credit: Alke Gröppel-Wegener).

straightforward; the promotional materials may frame the encounter *as* immersive, although whether each participant agrees that it was immersive afterwards is a different matter. Audience members might buy a ticket and be invited to turn up in a particular location at a set time, perhaps they are asked to put on a pair of headphones or VR headset, maybe they are even provided with some sort of costume or mask, and at the 'end' of the experience, to take it off. The markers of immersion here are physical, environmental, and now even ritual; participants in such encounters will know to expect immersion and, increasingly, will understand how to perform their immersion as well. In the second kind of practice referenced above, the boundaries are perhaps less clear and the moment (or moments) of immersion more difficult to ascertain. There are storyworlds that are tightly controlled when it comes to their visual and narrative appearance (such as the *Harry Potter* storyworld, the example we are employing in Chapter 2), but there are also storyworlds that embrace a more fluid approach, particularly when the creators change regularly as is the case in some comic book franchises, where complete reboots and changes in appearance seem to be almost commonplace. These storyworlds are also examples where fashioning your own props or taking part in CosPlay or LARPing might be appealing. By focusing on 'immersion', we foreground the embodied, performative, and experiential dimensions of interactions with these storyworlds in a way that the term 'transmedia' (for example) does not do sufficiently for our purposes, and we are not the first to work across these types of immersion in tandem. According to Anne Mangen's helpful distinction, the first of these practices might be understood as a form of 'technological immersion' in that it is crafted and *might* involve the use of tools, whereas the latter is perhaps more closely aligned with 'phenomenological immersion' in that it relies on our mental acts of imagination and cognition (Mangen 2008). This mirrors Wolf's distinction between 'physical' and 'sensual' immersion and what he terms 'conceptual' immersion (2012: 48).

For us, there are a number of characteristics that unite both of these types of practice under the banner of 'immersive storytelling', echoing scholars in this field introduced above. Firstly, they are audience and (often) participation centred. Secondly, each is at its most impactful when it is experienced as viscerally affective and every effort is made by designers to maximise the likelihood of such affects. Thirdly, each example of immersive storytelling is uniquely attuned to its contexts. Lastly, and importantly for our purposes here, both practices are story-led. These characteristics are echoed in the framework we introduce in this book, which explores how story emerges at the interstices of the creative process, the creation itself, and the experience of participants. We introduce the detail of these 'Orientations' in Chapter 2.

Overview of the Book

Having established our parameters in this introduction, we now offer an overview of our approach and arguments presented in the book.

18 *Introduction*

Research design in the realm of the experiential, the embodied, and the locative is fraught with complexity. Immersive contexts raise practical and ethical considerations for researchers and evaluators that we are only beginning to consider. In this book, we use our experiences as action researchers creating and evaluating immersive encounters to understand the logics and challenges inherent to immersive experiences. We reference scholarship from disciplines as diverse as media, games, theatre, theme park design, human computer interaction, and museum studies to make sense of the quality of immersion.

Chapter 2 introduces one approach to the analysis of immersive storytelling experiences and storyworlds, an approach that underpins discussions and data presented in the chapters that follow. As Farman ponders: 'What kind of story can a particular medium tell? What are the medium's affordances or constraints for telling stories?' (Farman 2015: 106). We introduce a framework that explores just that by focusing on the layers of each experience as a way of thinking about stories and storyworlds, and how they shift and migrate. In order to make our framework systematically sound, we start from a notion of experience that is somewhat broader than experiences that *have* to include story or that *have* to be immersive, let alone deliver deep immersion. In order to illustrate our framework, which we have termed the 'Layers of Experience' framework, we draw on a variety of ways of telling a story that are all located within one storyworld: the Wizarding World of *Harry Potter*. We explore the production of immersion through the franchise's varied textual and illustrative forms, filmic and theatrical genres and the themed lands,[7] as well as considering their analogue and digital dimensions, and mapping other extensions of the narrative up to the present day. Using one storyworld gives us the opportunity to not only demonstrate how to analyse one storytelling genre but also consider how a number of genres centred on the same story can work together to build a multilayered, immersive storyworld. For readers not familiar with this storyworld, we have prepared a section in our Glossary that gives an overview of the examples we are referring to, although it should be noted that this is not an attempt to map the whole of this storyworld completely, as this is far beyond the scope of this book.

Chapter 3 puts this 'Layers of Experience' framework into a practical context by applying it to one case study. The case study used here – ***Traces / Olion*** (which we will mostly just be referring to as ***Traces***) – is an immersive storytelling experience that we have had unique access to over the course of this writing project. First we introduce *Traces*, before offering an overview of the production process, ambitions, and principles that underpin it. We then present an analysis of participant responses to this experience of immersion, exploring the extent to which those who participate in immersive experiences are able and willing to co-produce and direct them, and whether agency within such encounters is practicable or desirable. We demonstrate that what constitutes an immersive experience can differ wildly depending on individual inclinations and contextual circumstances.

Chapter 4 then draws the lens back to take stock of immersion in its larger contexts. It introduces arguments *against* 'the immersive turn' in cultural narratives and experiences. These arguments focus on (for example) a perception of participatory spaces as in reality tyrannical and oppressive, and the promotion of 'experience' as a cynical tool of marketers and public relations. The chapter uses the concepts of 'aesthetic capitalism' (Murphy and de la Fuente 2014) and 'the experience economy' (Pine and Gilmore 1998) to frame these debates. Here, questions about agency, ethics, banality, and replication take centre stage. We conclude, however, that this is a more ambivalent process than some scholars have posited. For Mikhael Tara Garver, immersive media offer precisely a countenance to the 'hierarchical interaction' that we encounter in many other of our cultural interactions and can be considered as in some ways empowering (in Bucher 2017: 81). Immersive storytelling can reconnect us and offer us the kind of intimacy that other everyday spaces in our lives do not, workplaces and social media sites for example (Machon 2013: 26). Indeed, what emerges is a desire amongst many practitioners to connect to and consider questions about social justice, representation, and politics, and a hope that such practice can prove transformational. As Jason Farman notes, immersive storytelling *can* make previously marginalised stories visible, increase empathy, and engage people with place in ways that are fundamental and consequential (Farman 2015). As indicated here, there are 'political, aesthetic, cognitive, and ethical questions that are embedded within immersive forms' (Dinesh 2016: 2) and we discuss them in this chapter.

In Chapter 5, we offer a number of concluding reflections on the relationship between experiences, story, and immersion drawing on the themes raised in this introduction, and throughout the book. We consider their interplay and intersections in both the context in which we are likely to find immersive storytelling experiences, and in how we can approach them as researchers.

This book – which was always intended to be a short one – is the first to look across the diverse fields invested (and investing) in immersive storytelling experiences. It does not look at each of those fields in turn to offer, for example, a detailed introduction to and analysis of VR, or theme parks, or immersive journalism. Its ambition is bolder than that: to look across these evolving fields and to find touch points so that immersive storytelling can be articulated as itself a practice we can systematically explore. We use a detailed case study, and lots of examples, to illustrate our discussions. These examples are drawn internationally, and more information can be found about them in the Glossary, often including a weblink so you can find out more about them if you so wish (entries in the Glossary are indicated throughout in bold type). It is likely that at least some of these examples will prove ephemeral or be rendered obsolete in what is a rapidly evolving landscape. But we anticipate the debates they shine a light on will be with us for quite some time to come. Immersive storytelling continues to be fertile, instructive, and sometimes contentious terrain, as we will go on to demonstrate.

Notes

1 Examples highlighted in bold correspond to entries in the book's Glossary.
2 Originally published as *Die Unendliche Geschichte* in 1979. It should be noted that there are significant differences between the book and the 1984 film adaptation (and later sequels).
3 We have since spotted copies of *The Neverending Story* in paperback, with a different cover and using only black type. Unless they have changed the content slightly to make the links to this physical appearance coherent, the experience of reading them will probably be less immersive, as this link to the physicality is lost. How sad is that?
4 *Breathe* is also connected to the Ambient Literature project (Ambient Literature 2016).
5 Both of which we will refer back to in Chapter 4.
6 Our approach echoes that of Kelly McErlean (2018).
7 Themed lands are the different areas that usually make up a theme park.

2 Layers of Experience

As we have already begun to demonstrate, there are many different ways of telling a story that could be considered immersive (to varying degrees). The experiences we are concerned with here are, by their very nature, multilayered. Not necessarily in a physical, literal sense, but rather conceptually. They stand or fall in their successes based on whether all the layers work together – or how easy it is to simply ignore the layers (or aspects) that don't work for us as audience members or participants.

In order to explore this systematically across different interests and foci, in this chapter we present a framework that helps researchers to critically encounter and analyse storytelling experiences, by teasing apart their layers and examining them one by one. This gives us a way of establishing and articulating which storytelling experiences can be considered immersive, and on what basis. It also allows researchers to narrow their focus, specifically stating which layer(s) they are concentrating on as they investigate their own research questions located within the context of immersive storytelling experiences.

None of the theoretical frameworks we were familiar with allowed us to explore immersive storytelling in the way we imagined would be most helpful, that is, in considering all of the characteristics we identified in the introduction as integral to experience. Theories of remediation, for example, do not offer the granularity of perspective on participation that we require for our purposes in considering genres such as immersive theatre or street gaming. The same might be said for studies of transmedia, which pay their closest attentions to the (inter)texts themselves and the storyworlds they facilitate. Adaptation studies, while looking at the retelling of stories in different media, is not a homogenous field, instead spread over multiple disciplines with their own approaches (Elliot 2014: 71f), and as such does not provide a unifying framework.

22 Layers of Experience

Robert Stam for example provides 'an analytical/practical **model** for addressing actual adaptations' (Stam 2005: 32ff, original emphasis) but his focus on the filmic adaptation of literary works is too specific for our purposes. Scholarship on world-building and theme parks is intriguing, but its focus on entertainment and consumer spaces, and especially their physicality, is again not broad enough for our ambitions here. Conversely, scholarship on Virtual Reality (VR) and computer gaming does not pay enough attention to the physical and networked realities of (for example) transmedia storytelling. For example, the framework for immersive virtual environments sketched out by Slater and Wilbur (1997) is too focused on the technological environment it was developed for to be applied to experiences beyond the digital. The four realms of an experience[1] suggested as part of the experience economy paradigm by Pine and Gilmore (1998) is again a helpful model, but the economic background it has been developed against is problematic for our purposes (we return to this in Chapter 4). Pine and Gilmore also locate immersion and absorption at opposite ends of a spectrum, which seems to suggest that immersion cannot be absorbing, which we disagree with (playing an escape room, for example, can be both absorbing and immersive). Similarly, the five 'strategic experiential modules' that Schmitt (1999) cites as part of his experiential marketing approach overlap some of the aspects we present as important in this chapter, but don't quite allow us to consider the nuances and layers of the storytelling experiences we are interested in.

The theoretical framework that came closest to what we wanted to do was the Orientations of Genres framework developed by Fiona English (2012) in the context of her work on genre and regenreing. By identifying four different orientations of genres, English found a way to compare different genres in a systematic way, and therefore was able to discuss their affordances and the ways in which they differ (gains and losses). Lukas does something similar in *The Immersive Worlds Handbook* (2013). He argues that 'An important idea to consider is how telling a story in a three-dimensional architectural space is different from telling a story in text or in oral forms' (Lukas 2013: 52f). So he considers genre, even though that is not the term he uses.

This chapter starts by summarising English's work briefly and then uses it as inspiration for our own framework that is more appropriate for the requirements of immersive storytelling experiences, and which focuses on the concepts of *participant*, *process*, *creation*, and *story*. What we basically suggest is to 'explode' the examples we encounter, to investigate their different layers and look at those one by one to be able to describe, analyse, and evaluate them – first on an individual basis, and then in the complexity of the whole. In the development and discussion of these layers, we will make reference to and draw from the previously mentioned areas of scholarship where appropriate.

This approach allows us to look not only at the individual, bounded experience, but – if we are interested in a storyworld – to compare the different layers across the genres of said storyworld and consider how (or if) they complement each other. We will apply this in the context of an exemplar analysis in the next chapter; for this chapter, however, we are going to use examples from one specific storyworld to demonstrate the similarities and differences of various storytelling experiences: genres that have grown out of and extended the stories of *Harry Potter*.

Harry Potter has been chosen as an example not just because it is a well-known story, but because while it very clearly originates as a written text (the seven original novels), since its original publication it has taken form in many different genres that have truly extended it into a storyworld. This franchise has a variety of textual and illustrative forms, has made use of both filmic and theatrical genres, and has been made 'real' as multiple themed lands. The original narrative has been extended into a complex world that takes it far beyond both that original narrative, and the original creator J.K. Rowling. As such this immersive, and expansive, storyworld serves as a useful fount of examples for genres that can typically be located in the context of storytelling experiences.[2] For some information on the different examples we draw on, see the dedicated section in the Glossary.

The framework that we are going to present provides one suggestion for how to analyse a storytelling experience, and in so doing helps us to define 'immersion' and what we can judge as immersive. The Orientations of Genres framework we are basing this on was developed by English (2012) in the context of linguistics. English was not looking at immersive storytelling, but at storytelling of a very different sort: her work explores traditional and nontraditional academic genres and the process of turning one genre into another (a process she terms regenreing) as a pedagogical resource. English's framework provides a starting point for us, an approach that we can use, even though we are setting out in a rather different direction. While the examples she analysed were all genres that were written, the genres we are looking at in the context of immersive storytelling are not limited to words on page or screen. Immersive stories can be created through words, visuals, sounds, kinaesthetic experiences, through touch and even taste.

Using a different genre allows different ways of working with the material. For example, in words on a page you can describe the feeling of flying on the half-horse, half-eagle creature that within the *Harry Potter* storyworld is a Hippogriff. In a film, on the other hand, you can show it – but here it becomes externalised, you cannot show what Harry is feeling while flying on one, which you might tell in a novel. Using stereoscopic (3D) technology [and some of the later *Harry Potter* films had sequences in 3D on release, while only the last one was released in a full 3D version (Boucher 2011)], more of a flying experience might be felt by the audience, although they are still sitting statically in their auditorium seats. When playing the corresponding video game, gamers don't fly, but control a protagonist who is. In a theme park, however, riders themselves can experience 'flying'. While the '**Flight of the Hippogriff**' ride does not allow you to climb onto an actual Hippogriff and go flying on it – instead you are sitting in rather traditional roller coaster carts – the speed the audience is experiencing makes this both a kinaesthetic and visceral experience.

The different genres in which a story is told thus facilitate different kinds of experience. But which of them might be considered 'immersive'? In order to discuss this, we need to analyse the separate genres carefully, and find a way to break them systematically into their respective layers, which is where this framework comes in.

What Do We Mean by Genre?

Before we go further in exploring this framework, we first need to define what we mean by 'genre'. Here, we follow English's definition and approach to this concept.

> The special thing about *genre* is that it tells us that we are talking about 'texts'; that is, things that are produced with the intention of communicating meaning. [...] It also tells us that these texts are in some way classified into particular types. The term can be used to refer to the conceptual framing itself as in 'genre theory' or 'genre pedagogy', but when referring to actual texts genre is associated with identification, both of the text and of the participants in the textual practice.
>
> (English 2012: 68, original emphasis)

So, when we are talking about genre here, we are not particularly concerned with whether a story can be found under 'Fantasy' or 'Young Adult Fiction' in a bookshop. That is but one use of genre as a classification: looking at the broad themes of the content (which we will come back to in the section 'Topics and Themes' below). We are instead interested in the specific shape each telling takes, which rules it adheres to, and which opportunities each of these shapes, these genres, has. The genres (or formats) we can locate within the *Harry Potter* storyworld include (amongst others) novels, feature films, a play in two parts, video games, merchandise, and themed lands. We can group them into these genre types because they are pretty broad terms and we can reasonably assume that other people are familiar with their 'rules'. As English explains, 'Genre naming is useful in that it offers a shorthand means of referring to textual products without having to go into long and complicated explanations' (2012: 68). We assume that people will know what we mean when we talk about reading a novel: we are presumably referring to reading a book either alone or to/with somebody else. When we are talking about a play, we assume that people will be able to understand that while this exists in script form, the script is different from the play being performed. **Harry Potter and the Cursed Child**, for example, was widely sold in script form, which is quite unusual, as play scripts are commonly only purchased in the context of producing or analysing a play. But when reading the play script, people would have been aware that different rules are at work in this type of writing than in a novel, even though it is also presented through words on paper. Dialogue is presented differently. Stage directions appear that are written in a very different way than a description would be in prose. Its layout is different. We also understand that the play's script is only a part of what makes the genre of the play, because a play is performed by actors, and it often needs stage, costume, sound, and lighting design for example.

As English argues, genres communicate, they 'allow us to predict the kind of experience the text will provide' (2012: 69). For example, English has been using the term 'text' in the quotations presented here, and while some people might consider 'text' a genre in itself (namely a piece of work that exclusively contains written words), within the academic community, a 'text' can be understood as any cultural artefact chosen for study, whether textual or otherwise. This is how English is using it, how we are using it, and within the context of a book written for an academic audience, we have made the reasonable assumption that readers will be familiar with that convention.

> In a very general sense, I am using *genre* as a category which identifies the shape of a text, or better the framing of a text. It identifies what kind of text it is, that is what to expect from it, and at the same time, it shapes that identity. […] So now we can say that *genre* is a term which identifies texts as belonging to a particular type.
>
> (English 2012: 77, original emphasis)

There is a criticism within genre theory, most popularly flagged by Jacques Derrida, that defining a genre means putting too many rules on a text: 'As soon as the word "genre" is sounded, as soon as it is heard, as soon as one attempts to conceive it, a limit is drawn' (Derrida 1980; see also Abbott 2008; English 2012). We acknowledge that limitation, and use it as a starting point for critique within our framework. English put forward the notion of the affordances of genres because she was particularly interested in how the chosen genre changed not only the content of her students' regenred work but also their positioning as authors (English 2012: 66). She wanted to 'concentrate on what genres do' (English 2012: 66), their affordances, and this is also what we are interested in – how do the different genres communicate a story, and how can we articulate what they 'do' in the (story)world?

Our framework offers a robust mechanism to shine light on the layers of experience afforded by different genres, and in varying contexts – and of how immersion grows out of these layers and out of how these layers work together; as we noted in the introduction, in the right circumstances, a novel can lead to an immersive experience, but not every novel affords that to every reader. This framework allows us to explore why that might be.

Our Framework

In our framework, we concentrate on the layers storytelling experiences are made up of. However, not all experiences include all possible layers. A novel, for example, doesn't have an audible soundtrack. It might describe sounds, but the sounds are not actuated by the genre of a novel. An audiobook, on the other hand, does include an audio experience that could be explored further, but what it doesn't include is the visual layer a novel has (and we are not just talking about illustrations here, but the chosen typeface and layout, for example). So even though the actual words contained within these two genres – book and audiobook – might be exactly the same, the layers that make up the experience of engaging with these two genres are very different. And some layers are not found in both of them. This means that our proposed framework is inherently flexible, as we will be discussing layers that don't apply to all genres, and you will be able to see this in our example of applying the framework in Chapter 3.

As there are rather a lot of these potential layers, we need a way to organise and group them. Because the aspects that we are most interested in do not really fit into the framework proposed by English,[3] we are not utilising hers. Instead we are proposing our own, although we are keeping her notion of 'orientations' as an organising principle, which we will break down into the different 'layers' of the experience.

Our orientations are:

- *Participant* – where we are interested in the roles, identity, and agency of the people participating, whether that be as audience, users, guests, etc.;
- *Process* – where we are interested in the development of the story, and the experience and role of the people who 'tell' and 'make' it, including both original 'creator' and others involved in its production;
- *Creation* – where we are interested in how the story is told amongst other things through space and the senses;

and at the intersections of all of these orientations we have:

- *Story* – where we are specifically interested in the properties of the story told and experienced.

The story orientation differs slightly from the others, in that while all of these overlap to a certain extent in order to create a storytelling experience, it is the story that overlaps them all. We could best visualise this as a Venn diagram (Figure 2.1), where the story orientation can be found at the overlap of participant, process, and creation.

But where can that most elusive notion of the immersive be found in this context (and indeed in this framework)? Some layers will have the potential for delivering immersion, for example in a

28 *Layers of Experience*

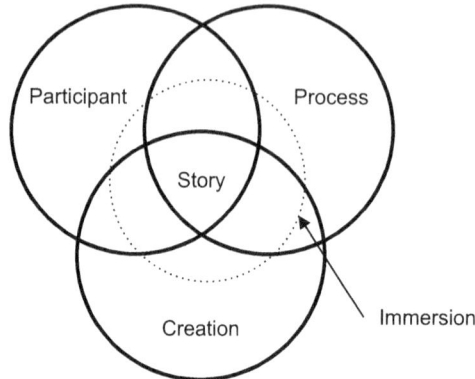

Figure 2.1 Layers of Experience overview.

physical sense – and we are flagging up what to look out for. But really experiences only become immersive when the different layers fit together and line up in just the right way. In other words, whether a storytelling experience is immersive for its participants is a judgement that can only really be made when all layers within the orientations have been considered. So immersion encompasses all in this framework, like a bubble forming within our Venn diagram.

Visualising the framework as a Venn diagram somewhat frees us from a hierarchical ordering of the orientations. In English's book, she visualises the Orientation of Genres framework as a three-tier bullet point list (English 2012: Figure 4.1, page 88). As has been argued previously (Gröppel-Wegener 2018), the way this is presented suggests a hierarchical order in a culture that reads from left to right and top to bottom. As a Venn diagram, it is easier to see the different circles denoting each orientation (participant, process and creation) as stand-alone entities, but also to see the overlaps between the neighbouring fields, as well as the story in the middle as literally central to our investigation.

In our framework, we present potential layers for investigation ordered by our three plus one orientations. While we are presenting them in an order, this is simply due to the linearity of the genre of the book, rather than to suggest a hierarchy between them. Depending on your own investigation you might choose a different order to discuss them, or even to leave some of them out altogether.[4]

We will now go through these orientations one by one, suggesting layers to be explored for each. We will give a brief definition of what

Layers of Experience 29

each layer consists of, followed by a few questions that researchers might want to consider as part of their methodology. As these can be quite abstract, we then use examples of genres drawn from the *Harry Potter* storyworld to illustrate these concerns. Given the focus of this book, we are not able to discuss all genres that make an appearance in this storyworld, and since this is not a book of *Harry Potter* scholarship we did not deem that necessary. Rather we have chosen examples that illustrate the different layers within each orientation best or contribute interesting perspectives on each layer and orientation, with particular reference to the immersive storytelling experience that this book focuses on. For more information on the examples, see the book's Glossary. Using one storyworld to draw from makes it easier to show the distinctions within and between the examples. We end each orientation with a brief reflection on its potential for immersion.

Orientation: Participant

The orientation of participant is concerned with the people that encounter the immersive experience or storyworld. These layers explore how participants become aware of and navigate the experience, what role they play within it, how they interact with it, and perhaps most importantly what they make of these interactions. We will look at participants' role and agency, their motivation, and practices of consumption.[5]

Participants' Role and Agency

Looking at the people who participate in experiences – and finding an appropriate lexicon for talking about them – is an important layer for us. While referring to people as part of an 'audience' for cultural encounters might be standard, calling them 'participants' suggests they have a more active role. Referring to them as 'consumers' provides a different connotation to the term 'guest' – and the term 'visitor' seems to suggest a different meaning still. There are no straightforward definitions of these terms, but this section suggests some of the questions that can be helpful when trying to define what the role of the people within a story experience is, and what is to be expected of them.

Theorists such as Walter Benjamin (1955), Roland Barthes (1977), and Marshall McLuhan (1964) have, over the years, posited that 'the distinction between author and public is about to lose its basic character' (Benjamin 1955: 225) and the notion of the passive consumer (Horkheimer and Adorno 1955) has long been challenged. Research has continued to demonstrate that audiences play an active role in their relationship with content, often rejecting or even boomeranging messages.[6] When considering participants, it is important to realise that they are not simply peopling an experience, but are playing a role within it – and within each genre they have certain powers (what we can call agency) as to what they can and cannot do or how actively they participate, and we need to consider that and this agency. Much immersive practice tends to explore that observation to its fullest. It is for this reason, and following literature explored in the Introduction, that we centre the term 'participant' within this orientation. It reminds us that immersion is not inevitable or a universal experience.

Some questions we might ask to explore the role and agency of participation within a storyworld therefore include the following:

- What is the most appropriate referent given the context? Examples include: Participant | Audience | Interactant | Visitor | Consumer | Player | Guest | Collaborator | Reader | Rider | User.
- Are they encouraged to adopt different roles at different points in the experience?
- How is the experience framed (if at all) so as to give them a sense of what will be expected of them?
- Does a participant move within the experience? Do they queue, sit, stand, or shuffle uncomfortably?
- What activities do the participants *have to* engage in, and what activities *could* they engage in?
- Do they interact with performers or one another? Are those interactions planned, scripted, or improvised? Who initiates them? Who decides when they end?
- Are those interactions meaningful, that is, do they have an impact on their experience, and/or the direction of the narrative?
- How do participants demonstrate their affective response to the experience? Do they scream, laugh, and shout? Do they cry? Do they leave in haste mid-way through?
- Does the role participants play help them to feel immersed?

A participant's role in the **Harry Potter novels** is very straightforward: you are a reader. Depending on the context, this might be a more involved experience, for example while reading the stories to children, you might choose to 'do' different voices for different characters, or not.

Within ***The Wizarding World of Harry Potter*** themed lands, the role of participants is in many ways a more active one. Here, you move through an environment and have many choices – where to go, in what order, and whether or not to purchase something, for example. Participants can be described as 'visitors' or 'guests' who walk, watch, hear, buy, eat, and drink. While you are not required to dress up and take on a role, you have the opportunity to do so – it is not uncommon to see people dressed in Hogwarts school robes. It is even possible to purchase interactive wands that allow the budding witch or wizard to cast spells themselves – if you perform a particular movement with those wands at a particular place in the themed lands, something happens. You might open a book in a shop window or command water to spew from a fountain. Of course this is all controlled by design and technology, but its aim is to facilitate deeper immersion in the storyworld. Your capacity for agency changes slightly if you decide to go on a ride, however. First you are herded into a queue where there are some, limited, opportunities for interaction. For example in '**Harry Potter and the Forbidden Journey**', the queue snakes through the castle and you can decide to linger in a room with portraits and paintings to listen to their conversations, if you don't mind losing your place in the queue that is. Once the actual ride starts you are strapped in and agency is (necessarily) restricted. That does not mean however that those experiences should not be understood as immersive.

Participants' Motivation

This layer explores how we might tease out the motivation of those who interact with a storytelling experience. While we can make some generalised assumptions about an audience, the motivation for each participant might stay a mystery unless we research that specifically. Here we might ask the following kinds of questions:

- Why does a person (or persons) choose to interact with this particular experience? Is theirs a genuine choice to become involved in the encounter?
- Is this framed by any previous encounters with similar experiences?

32 Layers of Experience

- Do they have an agenda as they interact with that experience? Are they hoping to enjoy, learn, win, campaign, or improve well-being, for example?
- Why is this particular experience or storyworld chosen over another (if it was chosen over another)?

Did you pick up one of the ***Harry Potter* novels** because you wanted to read it for your own entertainment? Because it was requested by your children as a bedtime story? In order to study it for a class? Or because everybody was talking about it and you wanted to know what the fuss was about?

Did you go to ***The Wizarding World of Harry Potter – Diagon Alley*** as the specific purpose of a trip to Florida, booking a whole holiday around it? Or did you want to go to Universal Studios Florida, and just happened upon it because it is one of the themed lands featured in this theme park? Maybe you live only half an hour away and pop in regularly if the weather is nice and you feel like it? Within the park, was there a particular ride you wanted to go on, even if the consequence was waiting in a queue for hours? Or was your primary motivation looking for some unusual pieces of merchandise to take home?

Practices of Consumption

This layer is concerned with the ways an experience is accessed by participants:

- Is it a solitary or a group experience?
- What is the time frame and duration of the experience? Is it repeatable, one-off, or is there a time limit? Can participants skip or repeat events/aspects/elements? Or is consumption incidental, even accidental?
- Does it take place in a specific space, or is it flexible?
- Is there a price – what is it?
- Is it a branded experience? How does that shape the experience?

Going to see ***Harry Potter and the Cursed Child*** can be a solitary or a group experience (and for the watching of the play itself, is there a big difference as there isn't really the opportunity to interact with each other?); it is repeatable; but there are also some limitations on how you can see it – because the official play is only performed in specific cities and on certain days, so both time and place are fixed to a certain degree. There is a ticket price, which depends on your seats, and there might be travel and possibly accommodation expenses.

The Immersed Participant

As we have seen, there are many aspects to consider when researching an experience through focusing on its participants: we can consider the reasons behind their choice to partake in the experience or how much time and money they commit to it, for example. Perhaps the most important aspect when it comes to judging whether an experience can be considered as immersive or not, however, is to look at the role of participants within it. As has been found in this orientation, there is a whole spectrum of agency and engagement that ranges from an active participant that has a lot of choice over how to behave and when to interact (like playing a character within a story), to a 'passive' audience member that gets physically immersed, but without much interaction or agency (like the rider of a themed roller coaster). Both of these (in some ways opposite) extremes can be considered immersive experiences once we explore the layers, although in rather different ways. The framework offers a language for beginning to articulate those assessments and differences.

Orientation: Process

This orientation investigates the process of creation, and those who have created an experience: for example the authors of stories, or the producers, designers, and engineers of aspects of a storyworld. In this orientation, the layers we suggest are the genre choice of the creators and their motivation for creation, the process they go through, as well as their identity and roles.

Creators' Genre Choice and Motivation

Possibly the most basic layer to investigate is why a particular genre was chosen by the creator(s) in the first place. Speaking to creators, reading their blog posts or interviews in the media will tell us something about their motivations, but we should be mindful that there are often different (potentially conflicting) agendas at play that can make these complex layers to unpack, especially for creative outputs that have been produced in collaboration or filtered through a number of intermediaries (editors, directors, financial backers, agents, and the like). Questions that might help include:

- What genre has been chosen? Is it a genre many people will be familiar with, a conventional genre, so to speak? Is it a new genre, possibly a hybrid?
- Is the choice based on the creator's own preference? Or have limitations been imposed by an outside force, such as a client?
- Is the motivation amateur creative expression (which could include fan endeavours) or was it part of a (paid) job? Are there additional motivations related to activism or education, for example?
- Is the experience at proof of concept stage, an experiment, or a full (possibly commercial) release?
- Was it part of a larger project?
- Is the experience conceived of and articulated as an immersive story? Or as part of an immersive storyworld? If so, by whom and for what purposes?
- What other intermediaries have been involved in the value chain? For example, how is it being marketed and distributed?

The play script of **Harry Potter and the Cursed Child** is a collaboration between J.K. Rowling, Jack Thorne, and John Tiffany [although Rowling herself apparently 'didn't put pen to paper on that project' (Chitwood 2016)]. When the play was first conceived 'Jo already had ideas about Harry and his world after leaving Hogwarts, as an adult and a father, and she became intrigued by how theatre could bring his story to life in a different way' (Palace Theatre 2018: unpaged). The programme of the production also states that 'at its heart, we hope that the play reflects the beauty of theatre – the simple art of storytelling in its purest form' (Palace Theatre 2018: unpaged). This suggests that the choice of theatre play as a genre led to the development of this part of the *Harry Potter* canon, combined with the purpose of continuing the story started in the novels. But since it was conceived as and written to be experienced as a theatrical production, the requirements of this genre shaped the final outcome.

The **Harry Potter: A History of Magic** exhibition saw a team of creators (in this case mainly British Library curators) work together using artefacts to provide a broader context to the *Harry Potter* stories and showcase the folklore of magic in our everyday world, 'to celebrate the inspiration behind J.K. Rowling's own spellbinding creations' (Harrison 2017: 8). It was conceived as a celebration for the twentieth anniversary of the publication of the first *Harry Potter* novel, and fulfils the Library's educational remit also. It not only refers to historical documents related to the subject of the books, but also shows archival materials from the books' production, such as drafts, edited sections, and sketches, therefore demystifying the idea that books spring finished from the imagination of an author. ***The Making of Harry Potter*** is a 'studio tour' that in a similar vein allows visitors to peek behind the film-making process by showing production drawings and white card models, as well as some film wizardry such as green screen technology. Themed lands, on the other hand, are under less pressure to educate, their prime motivation being entertainment.

Creators' Process

Here we move onto a consideration of the process by which the creator(s) bring the experience into being. Questions that might be asked include:

- What process did the creator go through in order to create the part of the story he or she was responsible for?
- Are there any external considerations that inform and shape the design process?
- Was immersion an ambition? If so, how did that ambition shape the process?
- Did the process change along the way?

For the ***Harry Potter* novels**, J.K. Rowling as creator/author planned out the plot, researched some of its aspects, wrote and revised the text, as well as submitted it to a number of publishing houses.[7]

The themed lands were designed by the team at Universal Creative, which meant not only using the novels and films as source material to build ***Diagon Alley*** as a physical location but also making it fit into the area of Universal Studios Orlando that they had to play with. Add to that the specific genre of a ride, this process can be even more complicated, because for a themed ride to be successful, it needs to tie into the theme, rather than just provide a kinaesthetic experience (in which case it would be an amusement park ride). Thierry Coup, a senior vice president at Universal Creative explains about the originally planned '**Harry Potter and the Escape from Gringotts**' ride: 'We kind of lost track of what made an attraction really great.' (Kleinhenz, no date) Ironically this refers to an attempt to stay true to the published story, and the realisation that this would become a more exciting ride if it included a confrontation between Harry Potter and Voldemort at the end, even though this is not in the book. The new version needed to be checked by Warner Bros. and J.K. Rowling herself, prolonging the process of planning and building the final attraction and finishing the themed land.

Creators' Identity and Role(s)

Creators have an identity in relation to their creation, as well as certain roles to play. The identity could be thought of as a job title of sorts, although part of the identity is also whether the creation has been done as a professional or amateur, for example. Things to consider here are:

- How far is the creator the originator of the story or an adapter of somebody else's 'instructions'?
- What is the 'job title' of this creator?
- Is the creation done as part of professional work or as amateur? Or is the creator working as a 'fan' who reimagines somebody else's material?
- Who has ownership of the text? Who maintains the rights? How fiercely are those rights protected?
- Who has control over the creative direction?

Within the *Harry Potter* storyworld, J.K. Rowling's identity is that of author and originator of the stories and storyworld. While the first novel could have been considered to have been produced while her identity as author was as amateur, or maybe better aspiring, it is now certainly professional. Her role as author is as storyteller, the informer of what happens, the descriptor of the scenes. She also acts as producer on a number of genres, and she is famously a gatekeeper and controller of the storyworld, for example, she needs to approve changes in storylines of rides at the themed lands (Kleinhenz, no date). Rowling's ownership is visible and intertextual in all the genres. But there are other visible agencies that some of the genres include, and those are tied to Warner Bros. as the franchise holders of the movies (Nocera 2008). For example, **The Making of Harry Potter** is an exhibition and not a theme park, because Warner Bros. and Rowling sold that license to Universal. The copyright and trademarks within the storyworld are fiercely protected, as can be seen by the number of lawsuits that concern it (Kluft 2015).

Julian Harrison was the lead curator of the British Library exhibition, again a professional identity. His role was to lead a team that researched the folklore of magic, and selected artefacts to be exhibited, as well as interpreting them via exhibit labels and the catalogues. The catalogue published by the British Library based on the ***Harry Potter: A History of Magic*** exhibition (British Library 2017) includes a number of copyright notices which on closer inspection show that Harrison, a creator in the term that he was lead curator of the exhibition, does not have any ownership of this work, not even of the introduction he wrote.

Creating Processes of Immersion

In these sections, we have introduced questions that can help to explore the creative process and its ambitions. Key here, when thinking about immersive storytelling experiences in particular, is a consideration of whether, why, and how a creative process worked with immersion in mind. Perhaps the ambition is to connect a creative output to other outputs as part of a larger and more expansive immersive storyworld, or to produce a time-limited event designed to implicate people in a visceral and performative storytelling experience. That a creator decides actively to work in such a way tells us much about (for example) how they wish to position their work in relation to the broader cultural landscape, their artistic inspirations, or the ambitions of their funders. All of these aspects can be scrutinised and made meaningful within the framework and questions introduced here.

Orientation: Creation

The orientation of the creation looks at both the design and the manifestations of the experience. Lukas calls this 'a design story' which:

> is told in three-dimensional space, using architecture, design, and forms of material culture. It may also include actors, performance, and forms of technology. [...] the design story creates a world in which people can relate, interact, enjoy, and explore.
> (Lukas 2013: 52)

This orientation explores and detangles all these aspects. Here we are particularly interested in layers used to build up the space – whether physical, virtual, or blended – and how the senses are engaged. Our layers specifically are topics and themes, the treatment of space, and the senses.

Topics and Themes

An investigation of topics that are covered is helpful to put genres into context with one another. This is what is often considered 'genre' in common usage (is it a Western or a Science Fiction story?).

- What are the broad topics covered?
- Do any secondary themes run through the experience?
- Are these explicit themes or subtle features (Lukas 2013: 53)?
- How are these themes and topics reflected in the design choices? Do they offer opportunities for immersion?

The **Harry Potter novels** can be considered Fantasy and coming-of-age – or Young adult – stories. As Harry moves through his school years, other themes become apparent such as problematising race: pure bloods against half-bloods or people with no magical blood; the rights of werewolves, goblins, and house elves.

The **Harry Potter: A History of Magic** exhibition, on the other hand, is not a coming-of-age story, and rather than fantasy it explores the folklore of magic through historical documents and artefacts. It also exhibits process documents that J.K. Rowling produced herself while plotting, writing, and revising the **Harry Potter novels**, as well as illustrations by Jim Kay and Olivia Lomenech Gill. So we could classify this as a non-fiction genre. Similarly, **The Making of Harry Potter** is an introduction to production and design activities related to the feature films, with themes including props, costumes, sets, and behind-the-scenes looks. It doesn't immerse you in the plot of the film, but by stepping into sets and getting to investigate the process of making the film it tells the story of film-making in an immersive way.

Space

Another layer that can be considered is how the experience uses and is related to space. This is a very complex issue and we will first be dividing this into three broad categories partly borrowed from Fiona Wilkie (2002): where the location is flexible; where the participant is interacting in site-generic space; and where the space and experience have a deeper relationship. We will then consider some aspects of spatial arrangements.

SITE-FLEXIBLE

There are storytelling genres that do not encode space within them – the site at which you as participant choose to engage with them is flexible, it could even be considered irrelevant to the design of the experience. This means that the participant has agency over the space of the encounter:

- Does the participant choose where (in the physical world) to engage in the experience?
- What are typical ways to engage with this genre? Casual or turning it into an occasion?

The most obvious genres within the *Harry Potter* canon that are site flexible are the books and audiobooks, the films once released to DVD, Blu-ray or streaming services, as well as video games and VR experiences. With each of these genres, it is the participant that decides where and when to engage, for how long and how intensively.

SITE-GENERIC

There are storytelling genres that take place in specific spaces, but there remain spaces that are generic to that particular genre, for example it doesn't matter which cinema you watch a film in.

- Is the experience linked to a particular type of venue?

A genre that could be considered site-generic within the *Harry Potter* storyworld is the exhibition ***Harry Potter: A History of Magic***. It was designed to fit into an exhibition space, and although it would not be as easy to transfer it to a different venue as it is to play the film at different (and multiple) cinemas, the space itself is not designed specifically for it; rather, the exhibition is designed to fit into the space.

SITE-SPECIFIC/DESIGNED

There are storytelling genres where the space is part and parcel of the experience, when either the experience is located in a specific location or the space has been designed for the experience specifically.

- Has the experience been designed to fit a specific location?
- Has the location been designed and created for a specific experience?
- Is the chosen site a constructed or a natural environment?
- Does the chosen/designed site provide a sense of immersion, possibly via a sense of authenticity?

The Making of Harry Potter is very much an experience that has been created in a specific location – at the studios where some of the films were actually recorded. Part of the selling point of the experience is that visitors can see and sometimes interact with original sets and artefacts. This experience is so site specific that it could not be built in a different location and one could say it allows immersion in the movie-making process, although from an observer's point of view.

The themed lands, on the other hand, are spaces that are specifically designed for this experience, but they can exist in different locations, and indeed do. It is quite common to 'clone' parts of theme parks at different locations around the world, usually with some small differences in their layout and attractions. At the time of writing, *The Wizarding World of Harry Potter* can be visited at Universal Studios resort in Orlando (in two themed lands, *Hogsmeade* in Universal Islands of Adventure and *Diagon Alley* in Universal Studios Florida), in Osaka (*Hogsmeade* at Universal Studios Japan), and in Los Angeles (*Hogsmeade* at Universal Studios Hollywood). They are specifically designed to be immersive in the sense of a 3D environment that visitors can go into and interact with, and while they can be cloned in a new location, they would be difficult to move.

LAYOUT/SPATIAL ARRANGEMENT

While the visual aspects of the design will be referenced below, if we are discussing space, we also need to consider the layout and accessibility of the experience, if they are in a site-generic or site-specific/designed space. While video games and VR experiences are, as mentioned above, site flexible in their use of physical space, the *virtual* space that is created as part of them and that the player can interact with needs to be considered here, too, just as the overlap between physical and virtual space in Augmented Reality applications can be subject to analysis.

Layers of Experience 41

- How is the story arranged in space?
- What is the relationship between the audience and the space of the story?
- Are maps available, and if so, are they accurate?

The *Harry Potter: A History of Magic* exhibition was organised within ten rooms with a clear flow from one room to the next, but people were free to linger, skip, or double back. The first room was really more of a corridor, becoming an entrance with steps leading down into the rest of the exhibition where the theming became more distinct, like visitors were entering an enormous magical library (with open books 'flying' above their heads).

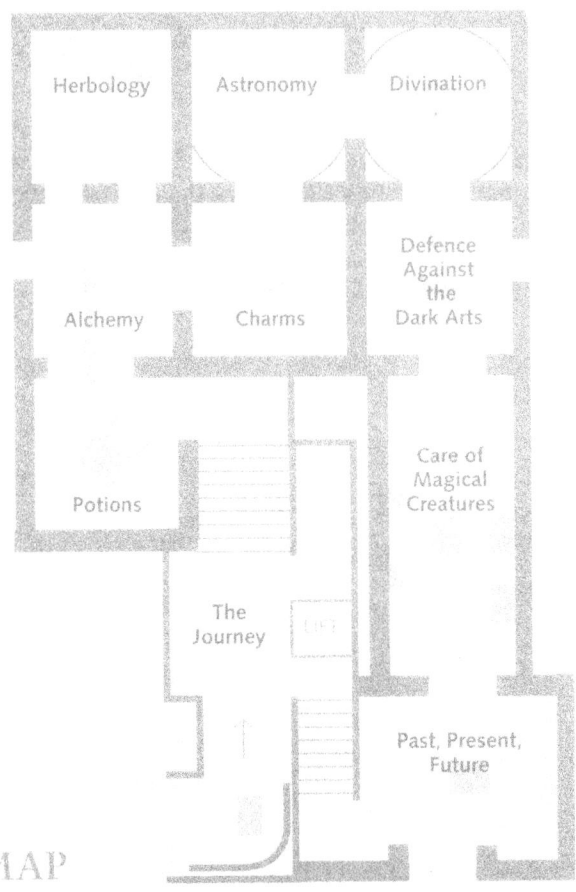

Figure 2.2 Map of *Harry Potter: A History of Magic* exhibition at the British Library (Credit: British Library).

42 *Layers of Experience*

Diagon Alley consists of two main sections: London like non-wizards would see it and the wizarding world contained behind it. The London section is very condensed and includes a somewhat scaled down replica of Kings Cross station where you can catch the '**Hogwarts Express**' ride to *Hogsmeade*, an approximation of Charing Cross Road and a part of Grimmauld Place (all locations featured in the original *Harry Potter* novels). This section is located within the larger context of Universal Studios Florida, which has the overarching story that it is a film studio, so these building frontages can be seen as part of a set and therefore appear realistic. The wizarding shopping streets of Diagon Alley, Horizont Alley, Carkitt Market, and Knockturn Alley, on the other hand, are accessed via two relatively hidden portals and remain enclosed – there is no visual 'leakage' from inside, you cannot look out into the non-wizarding world, in order to see the non-magical London, you need to exit Diagon Alley. Within this space, each attraction, ride, and retail outlet has its own space to occupy. The rides and attractions usually involve a queuing area that can be themed lightly or heavily. For the '**Harry Potter and the Escape from Gringotts**' ride, for example, the queuing area snakes through the entrance hall of the bank and down into its vaults. The idea behind theming the queuing area is to give visitors new things to discover while they are basically standing around – it is hoped the added details make the experience more immersive and reinforce the story that is being told.

The Senses

The engagement of more than one sense is often important in making an experience immersive. In this section, we look at 'modes' – a term that English defines as 'communicative channel[s]' (English 2012: 92) – and the senses they relate to. For example, books use written and visual modes; audiobooks use spoken and auditory modes; while VR experiences focus on visual, auditory, and sometimes kinaesthetic modes. This section proposes questions to consider for each of the most common senses and modes.

SIGHT AND VISUAL MODES

The visual can encompass a lot of aspects: from the graphic design and layout of books or posters to architecture, and from tiny details to macro-level overviews. There are a number of frameworks available to help analyse the use of visuals, for example Bertin's 'visual attributes' (Bertin 2001), the Gestalt principles developed in the context of Graphic Design (see Brownie 2006 for a summary; also see Gröppel-Wegener 2018: 31ff), and Lukas's suggestions when it comes to the building of immersive worlds (Lukas 2013). Some things that emerge as important to consider include:

- The size of and relationships between lines, spaces, buildings, artefacts, props, and the like.
- How is colour used?
- How is shape used?
- Is a visual style identifiable?
- Does the experience work in two dimensions or is it three dimensional? Are participants seeing the 'real thing' or a VR simulation? Do they need glasses or other equipment to access the full experience?
- How encompassing are the visuals?

When comparing the non-magical London section and the Diagon Alley enclosed part of the ***Diagon Alley*** themed land, just the way that colour and shape are treated tells visitors something about these different spaces. London is light and open, uses conventional architecture, clear symmetric shapes, and a fairly neutral colour palette. Diagon Alley (although also open-air) is much more enclosed, the buildings look mostly old and dusty, and although they use bold colours most of the shop fronts are faded, ageing them significantly. Here buildings mix a range of architectural styles, from gothic and castle-like to those clad in wooden slats or featuring Tudor black and whites. Overall there is a lack of right angles, which is subtle yet unnerving. Comparing these two spaces, London looks newer and almost clinical, whereas Diagon Alley seems quirkier and more established. The visuals of these spaces alone tell part of the story of how the wizarding world fits into – and exists alongside – the non-magical world (see Figure 2.3).

SOUND AND AUDITORY MODES

The play and interplay of different types of sound are hugely important in immersive storytelling. Lukas states that 'Hearing is a powerful sense because it can create a sense of a total space. It gives the guest all of the auditory cues that indicate where the person is

Figure 2.3 The *Wizarding World of Harry Potter – Diagon Alley* themed land at Universal Studios Florida contrasts a traditional London (top) with a much more colourful (if faded) and much more organically constructed wizard world (bottom) (Credit: Alke Gröppel-Wegener).

and what can be expected in the space.' (Lukas 2013: 197) Aspects to consider include:

- Is there discernable speech, and if so, is it part of the narrative or is it building the space (for example ambient chatter that suggests a crowded bar)?
- Is the sound diegetic (i.e. you can see where it comes from or understand where it comes from within the narrative) or non-diegetic (i.e. you cannot see where it comes from, such as soundtrack music)? Is the sound there to be noticed or to fade into the background?
- What is the soundtrack music like? Soft and quiet? Loud, fast, and dramatic? What instruments are used and to what effect?
- How is the sound delivered? Is it ambient or do participants have to wear headphones? Is it on a loop or triggered by an action?
- Does the use of sound make the experience feel immersive?

The themed lands use sound in a number of ways. There are areas where the soundtrack from the movies plays on a loop, which ties it into the storyworld and establishes where you are. There are some additional sounds that enhance the experience and story, for example hearing Moaning Myrtle in the restrooms at ***Hogsmeade***. Two of the interactive wand spells allow participants to turn a piece of music on and off. In one of the clothes shops, a mirror tells you that you look good when you pass it, giving the impression of enchantment and linking to something that happens in the novels.

TOUCH AND TACTILE MODES

The tactile dimensions of an encounter can often help to make it more impactful, resulting in more visceral and felt experiences. Here we also include thermoreception, as controlled temperatures can also play their part:

- Does the texture help define a space? For example, different textures on the ground of theme parks help tell the story of what environment and story you are in.
- What does the texture tell you? Do the textures recreate places? (Lukas 2013: 87)
- Does the temperature locate the experience in a time or place? Are temperature changes noticeable? Are they part of the narrative?

46 *Layers of Experience*

One big part of contemporary storytelling experiences that relies on touch is merchandise. Visitors can wear, eat, or otherwise use bought items on site, and preferably also take something home. The *Harry Potter* storyworld includes a multitude of merchandise such as robes, ties, scarves, and pins that identify the wearer not only as a Hogwarts student, but displays their allegiance to one of the school houses. Wearing merchandise is a tactile experience that can immerse visitors, literally enveloping them in the case of the Hogwarts robes.

The Wizarding World of Harry Potter themed lands have some noticeable temperature changes – once you enter the castle and the Gringotts Bank the temperature plummets. However, it is most obvious in Knockturn Alley, which is colder than the rest of the street area. These little details make a created world seem more realistic and immersive.

TASTE AND SMELL – GUSTATORY AND OLFACTORY MODES

Taste and smell are lesser used senses within storytelling experiences. However, there are experiences that focus solely on taste, such as wine tastings or themed menus, and most longer experiences have food and drink available, even if they do not focus on them specifically. Smell is an inherent part of taste, but can also be used on its own in a bid to increase immersion:

- What food or drink (if any) is available? Do these offerings tie into the larger story?
- Are smells attached to food or the natural environment (ambient, so to speak), or are they introduced artificially as part of the experience (such as in historic sites using smells in an attempt to recreate the past)?

Harry Potter experiences often include food and drink. Butterbeer, for example, is exclusively available at *The Making of Harry Potter* and *The Wizarding World of Harry Potter*. You can buy Bertie Bott's every flavoured beans, or non-magical versions of the skiving snack boxes the Weasley twins invented. The eateries at the themed lands offer some British classics, such as Bangers and Mash or Fish and Chips, which locate the experience in both (a version of) Britain and Rowling's magical world.

With foods come smells that consolidate experience, sweet smells when you are entering candy and ice-cream shops in the themed lands for example. But there are also smells that are not tied to food, the musty and mechanical smell of the '**Hogwarts Express**' for example, and the (hidden) spell for the interactive wands that allows you to smell dragon poop (Oh 2018).

PROPRIOCEPTION AND KINAESTHETIC MODES

Proprioception, the awareness of your body in space, relates to a number of issues already considered in the previous layer. There are genres where your body's location in space doesn't matter that much, as when you are reading a book or playing a video game. There are genres where movement is pertinent to accessing the story, for example in a promenade performance, where the audience moves from location to location (perhaps with some degree of choice). And then there are genres, such as some theme park rides, where the primary goal is the thrill of moving at speed. Questions to explore include:

- Is the participant moving or do they think they are moving?
- How much choice/agency do the participants have in the movement? Are they being moved?
- Is the movement a significant part of the story, or a way of getting from A to B?

The '**Harry Potter and the Escape from Gringotts**' ride at *Diagon Alley* involves a number of kinaesthetic layers. First, there is the queue that needs to be navigated. Here the visitors have little choice over the direction and the speed is usually dictated by others. The ride itself is a combination of roller coaster and simulator, meaning some time is spent in front of large screens, but that doesn't mean that you are not moving, because the vehicle might jolt. The 3D glasses you are wearing also help to simulate movement. Both these different experiences of movement – the queue and the ride – are integral to the story, working to provide an immersive experience.

SENSORY CONSISTENCY OF THE STORYWORLD

If you are interested in a storyworld, it can also make a difference whether the various modes are consistent over different genres.[8] Questions we might ask include:

- Are the ways the senses are engaged consistent across the genres, for example is the 'look' and the 'sound' the same?

48 Layers of Experience

- Does this consistency make it easier to feel immersed? Is any inconsistency irritating or feel like a mistake, making immersion difficult?

A lot of the *Harry Potter* genres reinforce each other. For example, the films, studio tours, and themed lands use the same imagery, and the creative process has been overseen by the same people. This makes places immediately recognisable: if you have seen Diagon Alley in the films, you have certain expectations, and it is a thrill to walk into it both at **The Making of Harry Potter** studio tour and at the **Diagon Alley** themed land. This makes it easier to feel immersed.

However, there are also genres that do not include this sensory continuity, for example the illustrated novels, where Jim Kay shows a very different version of Diagon Alley, or the **Harry Potter: A History of Magic** exhibition that uses historical artefacts and presents more diverse representations of magical elements such as the mandrake. The lack of sensory continuity in the exhibition emphasises its non-fiction-ness, in a way the British Library may see as a positive, yet it extends the storyworld in a rather different direction that some fans may feel more comfortable with than others.

The Immersive Creation

The creation orientation is the one where immersive aspects and potential are perhaps easiest to identify, as it is the orientation that considers the physical aspects of the experience. We have encountered two basic types of immersion. On the one hand, there is the individual genre 'interface' that layers different modes, building up from just one (for example audio presentation of an audiobook) to a full environment participants can walk into and interact with (for example the theme park). On the other hand, immersion is also built by the coming together of a number of different genres resulting in a consistent and cohesive storyworld. Both of these use layers to turn designed experiences into immersive experiences.

Orientation: Story

Where the orientations of participant, process, and creation intersect and overlap, we locate the story. But what do we actually mean by 'story'? As outlined in the introduction, this is one of the more problematic terms in this book. On the one hand, a story could be thought of as a series of events or happenings. But once we start thinking about *telling* a story, the term can be seen to take on different connotations. Suddenly it has an agenda, a message, a moral or lesson we want to teach, and is a way to connect with others. Story might also be considered as a mission or a design principle.

Larry Tuch has said that 'story is a key aspect of [an] immersive world. It's what gives the space *context* and meaning and it gives the guest a reason to be in that space' (quoted in Lukas 2013: 52). Storytelling can be so much more than just recounting a series of events. It is truly multilayered. Steve Alcorn notes in his work with budding writers that 'Plot is your protagonists physical journey. Story is your protagonists emotional journey. (...) the story will be how your protagonist changes inside' (Alcorn 2014). This is interesting in our context, because it hints at our approach of breaking things down into layers.

While we propose that the story emerges at the intersection of the previous three orientations, there are layers that we felt were best discussed in the specific context of story, namely the narrative and its 'backstory', the plot and linearity of the story told, characters and performance, as well as adaptive characteristics. We then move on to considering the immersive storytelling experience in its totality.

Narrative and Backstory

A narrative in its simplest form is about how information is given, how 'events' are told or developed. For some genres, having a narrator is very common, in a novel for example, or as a voice-over in a film. But other genres can also have a narrative, André Gaudreault, for example, adds to the telling of 'narration' the notion of showing ('monstration') (Stam 2005).

A sometimes hidden part of the narrative is the 'backstory.' This could be considered the larger context of a narrative, in terms of what has happened to the characters before this moment, but also in a larger historical and cultural sense. Backstory is an important element in the designing of theme parks, for example, where often characters are invented for the sole purpose of providing a cohesive narrative in an attraction, even if the visitors will not be familiar with it. It is this backstory that makes the created world believable and immersive. Backstory is also an interesting concept to explore when thinking about storyworlds.

50   *Layers of Experience*

When looking at narrative and backstory, there are a number of things to consider:

- Is this a story about how events are for the participant or for a (fictional) protagonist?
- Is there a narrator who explains what happens, what kind of narrator is it – first person or third person? Protagonist or witness? Unreliable, omniscient, or somewhere in between?
- Does the narrative unfold without a narrator? How does it do that?
- Is the narration a case of 'telling' or 'showing' – or a combination of these?
- Is there a backstory? A larger context that is told through details that some people might not even notice?
- If you are looking at a storyworld, do the other genres or versions of this story consider and strengthen each other?

The **Harry Potter novels** have a third-person narrator (Harry doesn't tell us directly what happens to him or what he is feeling, somebody else reports it); and mostly this is from a limited perspective as most of the storyline stays with Harry (a limited third-person narrator). However, particularly in the opening chapters of the novels, readers are told about things that happen for which Harry is not present, making the narration here omniscient. We can find a number of different backstories in the novels as characters recount memories, for example, and as the reader moves through the novels, the earlier ones become backstories for the later ones. There are other backstories, however, about the 'muggle' world for example, where very little action actually takes place. This is a backstory that is hidden in plain sight, because it is a narrative set in contemporary Britain. We also know that Harry was born in 1980,[9] and the books are set during the 1990s. There are, however, no real mentions of contemporary events or fashions. The other, much more pronounced, backstory is the history and culture of the wizarding world, and this is something that the readers find out about with Harry, who is also a new entrant into this world. Interestingly, this is what is now being 'filled in' via Rowling's writings on both **Pottermore** and in the **Fantastic Beasts and Where to Find Them** films, which are sometimes referred to as *Harry Potter* prequels.

The **Harry Potter: A History of Magic** exhibition has a very different style of narrative. It is not concerned with events as such, but information becomes woven into a story through the inclusion in the exhibition. The narrative here is provided in the artefacts themselves (showing) as well as in commentary via explanatory labels (telling) that establish a larger context. The narrators here are the label writers, the curators that researched and arranged the exhibition. As they are experts employed by the British Library, we can probably consider them as reliable narrators. This exhibition also includes what could be considered as backstory. On the one hand, it establishes the context to the novels by providing both select quotations from them as well as showing drawings and paintings from the illustrated editions. On the other hand, the whole premise of the exhibition is to build the context within which the magic in the books is made more believable in the everyday world, by introducing its folklore. By suggesting through its framing that this is how muggles have been getting magic wrong all these years, the exhibition provides a fascinating level of backstory for the whole *Harry Potter* storyworld, while using it as its own backstory at the same time.

Plot and Linearity

The plot of a story is what happens, and how the dramatic events that make up a story work in relation to each other. Plots can be analysed for their dramatic structure (and in different disciplines, scholars have talked about this in different ways, e.g. Freytag 1896; Propp 1971; Booker 2005; Campbell 2012), but the scope of this book doesn't allow us to go into this in detail. However, it is definitely worth looking at the plot, as well as the organisation of it, to analyse how a story is told, and how plot becomes a device for immersion:

- What elements make up the plot?
- How is the narrative organised?
- Is there a dramatic dimension to the plot?
- Is the plot made up of a fixed number of events in a specific order (i.e. a continuous narrative), or are the participants choosing the order for their own experiences (we could call this a modular narrative)?
- Is there a sense of chronology within the narrative, one thing has to happen in the experience to trigger something else?
- Are there different plots that can be built by alternative orders of events? Are there occasions where events branch into different plots?
- Does the plotted experience need to be consumed in one go or can it be interrupted and either continued or restarted?

The *Harry Potter* novels have clear (and fixed) plots. For example, the basic plot of ***Harry Potter and the Philosopher's Stone*** could be summarised as: orphaned Harry Potter finds out he is a wizard and starts attending a magical school. He makes friends, and enemies, and locates the Philosopher's Stone with the help of two of his friends, solving a number of challenges on the way, thwarting a villain. The individual novels are organised in chapters, but they also have an overarching order, which is chronologically following Harry getting older (one book for each year he is – or is supposed to be – a student at Hogwarts). These plots are continuous and meant to be 'consumed' in this particular order. However, readers have the choice whether they skip ahead or double back, as well as whether they read the book(s) in one go, or with breaks in between.

The ***Harry Potter: A History of Magic*** exhibition does not have a dramatic plot as such, but it is still conveying a story. Here the 'events' take the shape of artefacts and labels, as well as choice quotations from the novels to provide context. We can identify two different plots within the exhibition: the story of the writing and publication of the novels including new illustrations on the one hand, as well as the folklore that may have informed beliefs of magic on the other hand. These two plots are interwoven, although the exhibition starts and ends with the former, bookending the exhibition with rooms that exclusively contain artefacts related to the publishing phenomenon, such as J.K. Rowling's sketch of how the Hogwarts grounds are laid out in the first room, and a model box of the set for the play in the last room. The eight rooms in between are themed to represent subjects of study from Hogwarts' timetable. While the entry and exit points are fixed, visitors have the ability to follow these loose plots in the way they are set out, or pick and choose their own order. But once they leave the space, they cannot go back (except through the exhibition catalogues that organise the same plot elements in a different genre).

Playing the video games, such as ***Lego Harry Potter: Years 1–4***, includes elements and plots familiar from the books and films, and allows players to take charge of the order of the narrative themselves, at least to a certain degree. We could think of the plot here as modular: the elements are organised as little chunks, but it is up to the players in what order they are visited (as long as it is within the logic of the game). This also includes 'tests' of the players' skills and knowledge at some junctions – for example, if you don't put on earmuffs before handling the mandrakes, you could be in trouble, but if you do, you can use them to shatter glass. As with reading a book, players are also more in charge of the amount of time they spend playing. However, there is usually a certain order imposed by the game makers, such as particular tasks that need to be completed in order to move up to the next level.

Characters and Performance

The telling of a story also often includes characters, particularly if it includes a narrative. Depending on the genre you are looking at, these characters might be interpreted by performers in ways that confirm or challenge the initial interpretation. Some questions to consider are:

- What characters are there? Are they primary, secondary, and tertiary characters?
- Are they part of a narrative, or of a larger context, for example ticket takers in costume and/or speaking with a particular accent?
- Do the characters conform to archetypes?
- Does the genre include performances of characters (by people, audio-animatronics, or animations, for example)?
- Are the characters and performances unique to this experience or continued across a storyworld?

The ***Harry Potter* novels** include numerous characters – primary, secondary, and tertiary – and within the books they are described and the readers have to imagine them (unless they have encountered other media and artistic representations previously).

The casting of the original production of ***Harry Potter and the Cursed Child*** got some publicity when Noma Dumezweni, a black actor, was cast as Hermione Granger, a character that had been portrayed by Emma Watson, a white actor, in the films. J.K. Rowling explained that Hermione's race is never mentioned in the books and the best person for the job had been cast (Ratcliffe 2016). This was an interesting moment that raised questions about what consistency of performance actually means, and how its parameters are understood by audiences, often in problematic and simplistic ways. Subsequent castings of this role have also used black actors.

Adaptive Characteristics

The whole framework when applied allows us to see the differences between genres, and when applied to a regenred (or adapted) text allows us to trace the differences between original and adapted versions where appropriate.[10] This includes a closer look to how the different genres stand in relationship to each other and whether there is an original source that can be clearly identified (see Genette's notion of 'transtextuality' as explored by Stam 2005).[11]

- Is one of the genres clearly identified as the original source (which could also be called a 'hypotext' that 'hypertexts' adapt)?
- Do the individual genres reference each other, both with their narrative and their physical manifestations – and is this done in a way that shows consistency and continuity?
- If it is a straightforward retelling, what is gained and what is lost by switching genre?
- Does the focus of adaptations stay the same?
- Do the individual genres reference other stories (and genres) by alluding to or quoting them? Do the stories provide critical readings of each other?
- Do some stories develop the narrative of the original/the others?

For example, the feature films of the *Harry Potter* storyworld show a somewhat condensed plot from the novels, with slightly fewer characters and the occasionally altered (or newly invented) setting. But overall they provide a straightforward retelling of the narratives, and what they lose in plot because of time restrictions, they gain in the genre's ability to use visuals and sounds to tell the stories.

The Making of Harry Potter is not a retelling of the plot at all, and it references the films more than the novels. In this relationship, we could say that it is the films that have become the hypotext, the original, because this story is all about experiencing the film sets.

The **Harry Potter: A History of Magic** exhibition, on the other hand, does not reference the films at all, but makes links to the novels (and really celebrates them as originals). It is the one example discussed in this chapter that builds strong links with works outside of the *Harry Potter* world.

The Immersive Storytelling Experience

Looking at the layers that come together to create the story, and also all the other layers in the orientations that intersect to let the story emerge, it is now that we can consider the experience holistically to understand moments of immersion that cast participants as protagonists, that make them feel, and allow them to go back into the world (potentially) changed by their experience. As we have seen, it is the role and agency of the participants, the ambitions guiding the process, the environment (whether virtual or analogue) that the experience is set in, and the story itself, which work in combination and interplay to make a storytelling experience immersive.

In the final analysis, what matters is whether participants 'buy' into the experience and story – whether they commit to the story or not, whether they believe it and emotionally invest in it. At some level, where the majority of experiences are concerned, participants know that this is not part of their real, everyday life, and realise that this is something that has been created for them. The experience becomes a truly immersive storytelling experience if participants can suspend that knowledge. As Lukas explains:

> The suspension of disbelief, associated with Samuel Taylor Coleridge, is the idea that a person – whether engaged in a novel, a theme park ride, or playing a video game – willingly goes along with the story being told. Even in situations in which disbelief might get the better of the person and result in them pulling out of the drama being told, they stay with it.
>
> (Lukas 2013: 29)

This is a direct result of immersion. If not all details are right in the immersive world that has been created as part of the storytelling experience, it becomes easier for the participant(s) to be pulled back to the real world. Some experiences manage to suspend the disbelief of their participants more than others, making aspects of the created world believable in the moment, that wouldn't be under careful scrutiny. Consequently this is the last layer to consider, and it is the most problematic one, because how much a participant gets immersed in a story is difficult to predict and measure. And at least to some degree this depends on how much they can and are willing to forget about the real world.

- Is the story (and its created environment) convincing, or is a suspension of disbelief necessary? How is this handled and is it achieved?[12]

This is, of course, also an aspect of the genres within the *Harry Potter* storyworld, and it starts with the novels. As they are fantasy novels, a certain suspension of disbelief is required for the participants to 'buy' into this world – most importantly that there is a magical world that exists besides but not noticed by the non-magical world the readers themselves live in. The way this is handled is that Harry himself gets to know this world with the readers, and there are numerous mentions and incidences within the books that refer to the magical world taking steps to hide themselves from the non-magical world, with for example, spells that hide whole buildings and that change people's memories. So it is explained why we, as non-magical readers, are not aware of this world.

Visiting **The Wizarding World of Harry Potter** is a branded experience, in that the themed lands were designed to fit the visuals, sounds, and character interpretations introduced by the films. This means that these environments continue this already established part of the storyworld and seem to give visitors the opportunity to walk into the world itself – we could say that the wizarding world here opens up the 2D screen and allows participants to enter into a 3D environment, almost literally immersing themselves in not just familiar sights and sounds, but also in until now only guessed at smells, tastes, tactile, and kinaesthetic experiences. And while the continuity established with the films helps establish the buy-in, there are also aspects of this environment that don't necessarily work. For example, **Hogsmeade** village has been designed to be shrouded in eternal winter, complete with snow on its roofs (presumably because the **Harry Potter and the Prisoner of Azkaban** film features a visit of Harry and his friends to the village in winter). Considering the actual real-life location of these parks, certainly the one in Orlando, this results in participants that are in warm or hot weather interacting in an environment that looks like it should be considerably colder. This can result in disbelief and the participant snapping out of immersion.

Interestingly, breaking the immersion of a context can also be a part of the experience (and the genre) selected. As we have seen, both **The Making of Harry Potter** studio tour and **Harry Potter: A History of Magic** to certain degrees acknowledge this storyworld to be fictitious – and indeed are focusing on this. But does this mean they are not immersive experiences on their own? They might break the immersion of the storyworld as something that is 'real', but the stories they tell about the making of the films and the writing of the books and magical folklore do have the potential for immersion and contribute to the storyworld in their own way. These examples illustrate some of the complexities encountered when exploring what immersion means in the context of storytelling experiences, and flag up how crucial it is to take the relationship of the encounter to 'real' life into account.

Figure 2.4 The Wizarding World of Harry Potter – Hogsmeade at Universal Islands of Adventure has snow on the roofs, but not on the ground (nor slush or water either). If it is cold enough for snow, why are people strolling around in shorts and T-shirts? (Credit: Alke Gröppel-Wegener).

Summary: Using the Framework

This framework allows us to look at complex storytelling experiences layer by layer, to describe and analyse what makes up the whole. While it doesn't allow us to make general claims about whether or not something *is* indeed an immersive storytelling experience, it can help us in arguing why a specific experience *could be* considered one or not. It also allows us to compare different experiences systematically, whether in order to see their differences or their similarities, to judge if they add up to a cohesive storyworld. As we saw in the summaries of the first three orientations, immersive aspects appear in all of them, even if the creation orientation is probably the richest in its potential for analysis here. But they really come together once the story orientation is introduced, and it is only when seeing all the layers working together that we can consider whether the story experience has enough potential to be bought into by the participants it has been conceived for.

We believe that this framework can be used to help researchers formulate their research designs when investigating immersive storytelling experiences. While not every layer will be relevant for each experience, and there might be some out there that we haven't yet considered, we hope researchers will feel empowered to add and leave out layers to make the framework work for them. In the next chapter, we demonstrate its application to a specific case study.

Notes

1 The four realms of an experience in this model are passive and active participation, absorption, and immersion; in between them the 4Es (Esthetic, Entertainment, Education, Escapism) can be found.
2 However, what we are not trying to do is map out the whole of this storyworld within this framework, as it would go significantly beyond the scope of this book. To see the framework in action, see Chapter 3.
3 Neither do the points of comparison Lukas suggests (in Tables 2–4 Traditional versus Design Story, Lukas 2013: 53): Plot or Narrative, Perspective, Theme, Characters, Setting, and Reader, although we will be discussing most of these within the suggested framework.
4 And you will see that in Chapter 3 we utilise a different ordering than in the following discussion, offering our reasoning for doing so at the start.
5 It should be noted that a significant overlap exists between the participant and where the process orientation specifically looks at the role of the creator when it comes to fan endeavours such as CosPlay, fan fiction and films, parodies, and the like. Our framework is flexible enough to cope with these developments by considering the role of fans – while they were previously understood as audience members and occasional participants, they now can become active in aspects of production. However, in so doing, they turn into creators themselves, and our framework can treat them as such. Consequently, the participant orientation looks at people who are participating, while the following process orientation looks at people who are creating, and we fully acknowledge that fans might be found in both. See Jenkins (1992), Hills (2002), Duffett (2013), as well as Hellekson and Busse (2014) for more information on fans and fandom.
6 See for example Cooper and Dinerman (1951), Katz and Liebes (1993), Jhally and Lewis (1992), Gillespie (1995), Bobo (1995), Morley (1980), and Ang (1995).

7 Some of the 'process' documents were exhibited as part of the British Library exhibition and are reproduced in the catalogue (British Library 2017).
8 This is a concept borrowed from adaptation studies, although there it is more usually referred to as 'fidelity'. However, as has been pointed out by Stam (2005), 'fidelity' and 'infidelity' as terms suggest that there is a right interpretation, which isn't necessarily the case. 'Consistency' as a term is more neutral, which is why we have decided to use this instead.
9 While it is never directly mentioned in the books, this is the date that *Pottermore* uses and as such we can deem it as official.
10 We have already considered Sensory Consistency as part of the senses in the creation orientation.
11 For some more detailed issues to consider when you are working with the filmic adaptation of a literary source in particular, see Stam (2005).
12 Lukas suggests a list of the Top Ten Story breakers (2013: 212f) in the context of immersive environments.

3 *Traces*
A Case Study

While we tried to make the framework presented in the previous chapter less abstract by 'illustrating' the layers of the different orientations in the context of the *Harry Potter* storyworld, we were only able to provide an overview because of the scale of that franchise. In order to demonstrate the approach to an immersive storytelling research project more comprehensively, in this chapter we explore one case study in light of the Layers of Experience framework introduced in Chapter 2. The chosen case study is an immersive heritage experience called ***Traces*** (***Olion*** in the Welsh language), an ambient and lyrical storytelling encounter at St Fagans National Museum of History, Wales (2017–2018).[1]

In order to be as useful to researchers as possible, we have kept the overarching organisation of the orientations, albeit in a different order: First, we explore the orientation of the *creation* through the lens of an observational researcher interacting with the finished storytelling experience (in this case Alke, who had no involvement with *Traces* until the moment she put on her headphones to be a participant). Second, we introduce and analyse the orientation of the creative *process*, which gives us access to its ambitions as an immersive encounter. Here we take stock of the creators' process through the lens of somebody who was involved (in this case Jenny, who worked on the creation of *Traces*/*Olion* as the Cardiff University partner). Third, we foreground the insights that can be gleaned from detailed research with *participants* into the experience of 'being immersed', introducing data created through semi-structured interviews in the evaluation of the project (again, Jenny). Ordering the chapter in this way is not an argument for privileging one perspective over another, but rather a way of exploring the dynamic and multivariate ways in which immersion can be understood and articulated. As a preamble to the discussion of each of these orientations in turn, we include a brief introduction to the methods that we used in order to collect,

Figure 3.1 Traces/Olion logo (Credit: Hoffi/yello brick).

process, analyse, and review data associated with each perspective. In doing so, we showcase three very different approaches to research and research data, again to model possible practice.

Finally, we reflect on the ways in which *story* – and specifically *immersive story* – emerges at the nexus of these orientations (this section is co-written by the two of us as a summative reflection on *Traces* as an immersive storytelling experience). This demonstrates why the story orientation is located at the intersection of the other orientations. We will encounter brief nods to story and storytelling in each of the three sections, but need to draw from all of them in order to comprehensively reflect on *Traces* as immersive story. This also models the principle of triangulation – looking at the project from different perspectives in order to arrive at a picture that is as complete as possible.

Orientation: Creation

It can be helpful if researchers approach a storytelling experience by initially participating in it themselves. This section does just that, sketching out a research encounter that could lead to the formulation of more formal research questions, but also showing how many of those questions you can explore without consulting other participants. It shares Alke's narrative from the lens of participant as researcher, making sense of the experience, in particular its creation orientation.

Approach and Methods

The primary research for this section was done on 17 May 2018 conducting *Traces* as a partner walk, with Alke taking the 'Rose' option. What follows demonstrates an autoethnographic

62 Traces: *A Case Study*

reflection, detailed from field notes taken shortly after the end of the walk (see Figure 3.2), and written up into digitised notes within a few weeks. The next step in the research process was to listen to all versions of the experience via the app (it was not possible to repeat the walk for logistical reasons), sketching out the different routes and taking notes that focused on how and where the stories overlapped or diverged (also noted down on the map in Figure 3.2).

Collecting data from the perspective of *you* as part of the audience can be helpful as it gives you the option to add a personal perspective when disseminating the research. While this might not always be appropriate in an academic article, it could enliven a paper presentation at a conference, for example. It can really help *your* storytelling about the (storytelling) experience and connect with your audience. For example, in *The Immersive Worlds Handbook*, Scott A. Lukas includes a section titled 'field journal' where he briefly describes his experience of a particular themed space, in his case a restaurant (2013: 55). He later includes an interview with the creator of said space, but at this point doesn't have to explain what type of space it is anymore, because this has already been done. This field journal section also breaks up the theoretical and historical information on

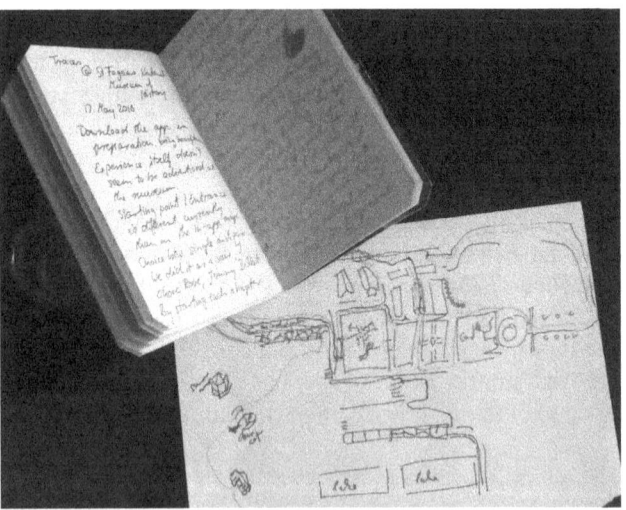

Figure 3.2 Alke's field notes from her *Traces* experience - handwritten bullet points and a scribbled map of how she remembered the experience shortly after taking part in it (Credit: Alke Gröppel-Wegener).

themed spaces nicely and is a useful counterpoint to general information in that it is so specifically focused on just one attraction, and one experience of it.

Findings: **Traces,** *an Introduction*

Traces/Olion is an audio storytelling encounter accessed through a free app, built to be experienced within the castle gardens at St Fagans National Museum of History in Wales. As a participant you have a number of options: you can choose the English language version, *Traces*, or the Welsh language version, *Olion*[2]; and within each of these options you can choose either the solo experience, or, if you are there with a companion, the partner experience. If you are choosing the partner version, you further need to assign each person a route by choosing either the 'Rose' or the 'Bullet' on the screen. Each option corresponds to a slightly different route meaning those who take the partner journey will be parted and reunited on a number of occasions during their encounter. The only major distinction between the single and partner journeys is that the single walk is designed for accessibility, while the partner routes include steps.

All these versions have a similar approach. The voice you hear through your headphones is your guide, the 'unraveller of threads', that takes you on a journey through the gardens and (notionally) through time. The topics and themes covered in *Traces* are closely tied to its location: participants get an insight into events that (may) have unfolded in the gardens, and there is a particular emphasis on the way the space was used as a convalescence hospital during World War I. An original musical score also accompanies you on your journey.

Your role in all of this is one of listener and walker. It is active in that this is a kinaesthetic experience – the movement from location to location is an important part of the encounter – but your guide tells you which path to choose. You are somewhere between active and passive, not just a recipient of stories but implicated in the narrative, asked to imagine things, recall memories, and interact with the gardens: close your eyes, touch the stones, leave a memory, trace a letter. Participation is at its most immersive when you are journeying with a partner. Here the stories are synced in a way that your partner becomes a character in your experience, and you in theirs. The narrator refers to your partner as you observe from a different part of the garden, and they seem to act out a part of the

64 Traces: *A Case Study*

story for you, becoming (for example) the character that clutches at the gilded gate staring longingly at the castle. At one point, you sit down opposite each other and close your eyes; yet, when the partner following the Rose route opens their eyes, their partner is gone. In another moment, you meet in the middle of a tunnel made of trees for a game of rock, paper, scissors, with your guide counting you in.

Traces was created specifically for the castle gardens of St Fagans. It is thus a site-specific exploration of the space, making use of features that have been in place for many decades, the gardens, vistas, paths, and gates for example. The narrator talks about the gardens, the mulberry trees, the steps that lead nowhere, and even incorporates the traffic outside a gate at the rear of the site into the narrative. *Traces* builds on the site's capacity to facilitate spatial immersion, literally in some locations such as within the tunnel made of trees that envelops you at one point in the story (see Figure 3.3), and it does so playfully at times also, for example, the narrative encourages you to avoid stepping on the cracks of 'the path of crooked stones', as one of the characters (a child) invisibly skips along and does the same next to you. It is as if you fall into step with them.

As the whole experience is outside, you are reliant on good weather or a sturdy umbrella. If participants are lucky enough to encounter the former, they might be tempted to go back and enjoy

Figure 3.3 Becoming immersed in a tunnel made of trees while exploring *Traces* (Credit: Jenny Kidd).

the gardens independently after the experience ends. Whilst smell is not something that is structured into the experience, depending on the time of year you are visiting, you may well encounter smell as part of a glorious sense-scape that helps build this ambient storyworld. In spring, the smell of a magnificent wisteria hangs in the air. Touch is also important in *Traces*. At a number of points, participants are asked to touch certain surfaces – the leaves on a hedge, the stones in an arch, or decorative parapets that line the stairways. Each time you are encouraged to reflect on that touch, and maybe even to leave something behind, as if you could transfer a memory into the stone. Depending on the weather, the stone can be cool or warm to the touch, and as you move from sunny areas to more shaded ones, or from summer into autumn, the temperature can alter dramatically.

The story could be considered the most challenging part of the experience. *Traces* is not linear, and it is not 'complete' in the sense of the traditional narrative arc. As the name of the experience suggests, you are encountering traces of stories that happened in this space, and traces of characters also. Participants become sort of observers of these characters by listening to fragments of stories about Agnes, Rose, and others, as well as seeing (and interacting with) the spaces they inhabited. You hear about these characters, but really only get a vague sense of who they were: Agnes is a little girl who was born there – but what happened to her when she grew up? Rose is a young woman left behind by a fiancé when he went to war. There is mention of her going abroad and being a factory owner, but these achievements are never explained; (former) soldiers convalesce in the castle and roam the grounds; you hear about a man with a dog and a love for riddles. These traces are intriguing threads that a participant might want to follow further, but there is no real sense of closure for them within the narrative itself. It is also not clear where they come from – are they made up, or were they real? Once at the end, you might wish to find out more about them through a display or similar – or to find out more by listening again and selecting a different option. Such endeavour would not be rewarded, however, as no more is revealed in the different versions.

This section has provided an introduction to Traces as an encounter, focusing in particular on its uses of space and sensorial interaction, its thematisation, and its use of characters. It has begun to hint at some of the challenges faced in the production of this immersive storytelling experience. That production process is the focus of the next section.

66 Traces: *A Case Study*

Orientation: Process

Approach and Methods

The following is written by Jenny as a member of the project development team. Involvement in *Traces* was for Jenny a rich form of ethnography (through immersion in the team over the course of the project) that allowed access to all stages in the process of scoping, designing, building, and testing a new 'product'. The *Traces* project itself was an action research project in that it featured a team collaboratively and reflexively working to create innovative practice, with a view to producing recommendations for others working in this field. The next section offers a detailed account of those processes – the 'findings' from Jenny's experience of immersion during that time – and is informed by attention to the layers for this orientation outlined in the previous chapter.

Findings: **Traces** *as Creative Process*

The *Traces* project was a collaboration between Dafydd James and Sara Huws at Amgueddfa Cymru – National Museum Wales (ACNMW), Alison John at yello brick, and Jenny Kidd at Cardiff University. This was not the first project this group of collaborators had worked on together: in 2013–2014, they had created a prototype immersive storytelling experience called **With New Eyes I See** which had been located in the vicinity of National Museum Cardiff (Kidd 2017; Galani and Kidd 2019).

Unlike more traditional forms of interpretation within museums, *Traces* is not a tour guide, an audio guide, or a mobile wayfinding application. The team wanted it to have a very different look and feel to these other genres, encouraging users to engage emotionally, to touch, and to become immersed. Immersion was thus a stated ambition of the project from the outset. We had seen in the **With New Eyes I See** project that immersive formats can connect participants viscerally and powerfully with history, place, and with each other, and wanted to push these possibilities further with *Traces*.

Traces was funded by a research grant from the UK's Economic and Social Research Council. The goal was for this to be a co-design process which meant that the design choices that informed the making of *Traces* were very open and the process itself iterative. The end product, however, was informed by the partners' own motivations for the project which usefully came into alignment on this project.

yello brick (the creative economy partner) was keen to explore further how its experience in games design and putting on immersive theatre events could translate into work with heritage partners. ACNMW (the heritage partner) wanted to broaden its experimentation with digital cultural heritage, and in particular, at St Fagans during a time of massive capital redevelopment. This was an opportunity to diversify the stories being told on site, and the ways in which they were being told. For Cardiff University (the research partner), this was an opportunity to deepen connections with partner institutions and to facilitate in-depth research with participants into their experiences of 'immersive heritage' (Kidd 2018a).

In the early stages of the project, members of the research and design team spent a day on site talking informally with members of the public and asking them to leave comments about the kind of digital offering they would like from St Fagans. People told the team that they were prone to following the same route through the site and seeking out familiar experiences visit after visit. They talked openly and enthusiastically about the sedimented, nostalgic, and emotional attachments they had with the site and this was intriguing. The team – after additional discussions with marketing, education, and curatorial staff on site – decided to produce a digital experience that embraced and worked with those feelings rather than one that provided yet more layers of interpretation, or a new interface for accessing existing digital assets.

The creative team on *Traces* featured a producer (Alison John), a tech partner to build the app (Hoffi), a Welsh and English language writer (Sara Lewis), a composer (Jak Poore), and an actor (Natalie Paisey). These different roles were all key to delivery of the project. The design process followed the existing yello brick model for working on a commission and features four stages: discerning the *audience*, deciding on a *location*, designing a *mechanic* for delivery, and working up the *story*.

The target audience for the experience was 20- to 35-year-old visitors who might be – and in yello brick's experience often are – inclined to seek out new cultural experiences such as street games, escape rooms, and immersive theatre, as well as repeat visitors who might be open to navigating the site in a new way. This was not an experience that would be targeted at children or families, so the writers could be more ambitious with the language, and the museum would not need to worry about unchaperoned children on the site. As with other ACNMW projects, and given their commitment to comply with the Welsh Government's Welsh Language Standards, there was always the intention to produce an experience for both Welsh- and English-speaking visitors. We wanted *Olion* to be more than a mirror translation of an English language version, however, and worked closely with the (bilingual) writer so that it would 'sing' in its own way (Huws et al. 2019). *Olion* thus had a separate work stream within the creative process, which is atypical for the Museum.

The decision about location was informed by the large redevelopment that was happening at St Fagans at the time, and the findings from scoping discussions with visitors that they overwhelmingly turn left when they enter the site. This meant that the part of the site featuring a now iconic row of houses illustrating life in Wales through the ages (on the left of the site) received many more visitors than the castle and castle gardens (on the right). Might *Traces* be a way of encouraging them to change their visiting habits and delve into the lesser explored parts of the site?

Decisions about the mechanics of the experience were informed by yello brick's prior work on street gaming and interactive narratives, and their deep understanding of the target audience from these endeavours. The idea of creating a branching and foldback narrative (Adams 2014: 227) that would split partners and reunite them for 'happenings' emerged early on. The decision to package *Traces* within the format of a mobile application was not straightforward. There has been quite some debate within the museum sector about the popularity and value of apps for users, and thus their return on investment. But St Fagans represented particular challenges that made a mobile app the best option for delivery of the project; connectivity issues on site meant that visitors would need to be able to access content via a self-contained experience, and not one that relied on GPS or mobile signal.

Decisions about story were probably the most challenging in this case study. St Fagans is a site rich in stories, and in other formats for interpretation. The team did not want to repackage, reiterate, or contradict existing interpretation through *Traces*, but to do something different instead, to be more playful in its approach. The research and design team spent many hours in the archives and exploring the spaces of St Fagans, unearthing stories and connections that could be enlivened in this project. Emerging from incomplete and often untold narratives the project developed into an artistic interpretation or composition grounded in those fragments; yet, it made no attempt to reconcile them into 'complete' stories. The narrative was designed to engage the senses also. It asks participants to touch, stop, and breathe in the landscape: the

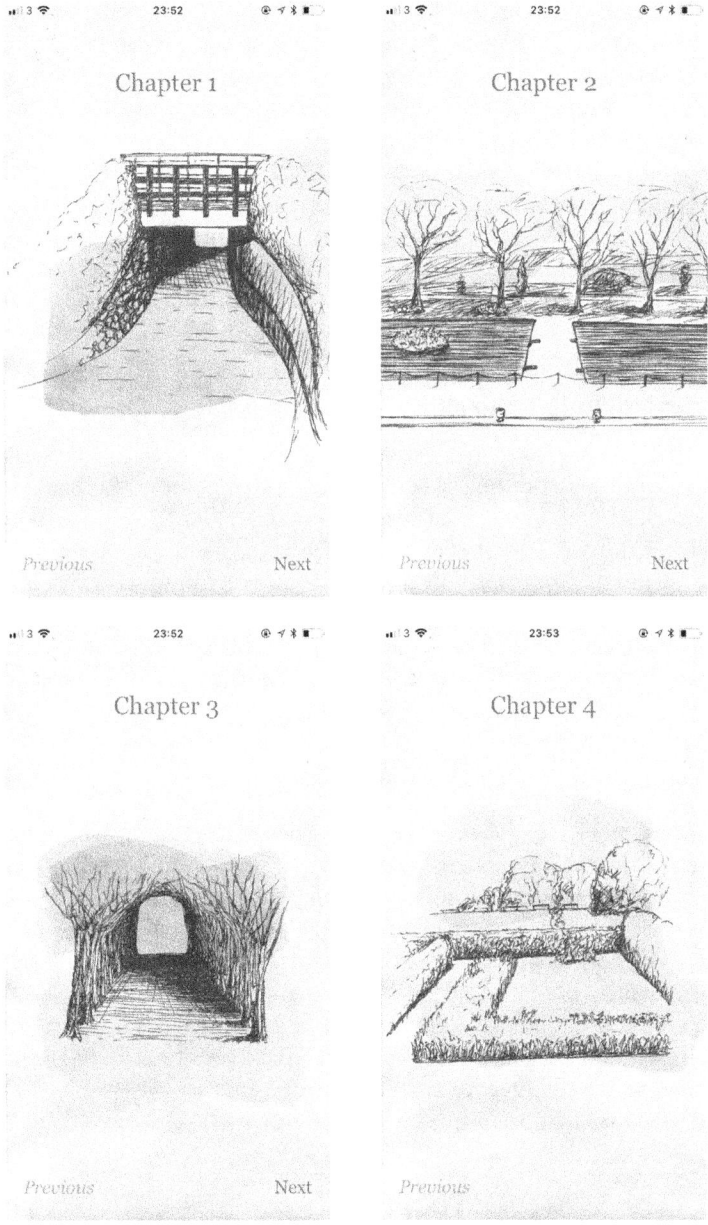

Figure 3.4 Sketches used in the *Traces* app show off the areas of St Fagans that the experience encourages participants to explore (Credit: Hoffi/yello brick).

smell of the gardens, the brush of the breeze, the chill of the rain. Towards the end of the encounter, they are encouraged to press their hands deep into the stone of the garden's walls and to 'implant' a memory there in order to become a part of this place, to change it, and to be changed by it.

Exploring the layers of immersion here – process, creators' genre choice and motivation, identity, and roles – means we are able to understand the ambitions for *Traces* as an immersive storytelling experience. We revisit these ambitions in the next section of this chapter in our overview of participant responses to this particular immersive storytelling experience.

Orientation: Participant

In order to explore what the patterns and practices of immersion were for those who took part in *Traces*, core members of the creative team (Jenny and a team of researchers from Cardiff University, as well as the Creative Producer of *Traces*, Alison John) embarked on an intensive period of research into participant experiences in March 2018. This data collection usefully coincided with the writing of this book, and was in many ways informed by it. The approach to this orientation very much takes the form of a structured evaluation (Figure 3.5).

Approach and Methods

As has been noted, *Traces* can be journeyed as either a two person/ partner or single person narrative. We wanted to make sense of how participants were responding to both of these journeys, and to begin to compare how immersion as a felt experience changed as the social dynamics of participation themselves changed. We worked with 12 individuals and 9 sets of partners (a further 18 people) who experienced *Traces*. In total then we had detailed research interactions with 30 people over a period of 3 days on site at St Fagans.

The research questions that informed our investigation of immersion and its possibilities were as follows:

1 What kinds of transitions, transactions, and thresholds make processes of immersion possible?
2 How does it feel to be a participant in an immersive experience? And how can researchers fruitfully explore the affective dimensions of immersion?

Choose your journey

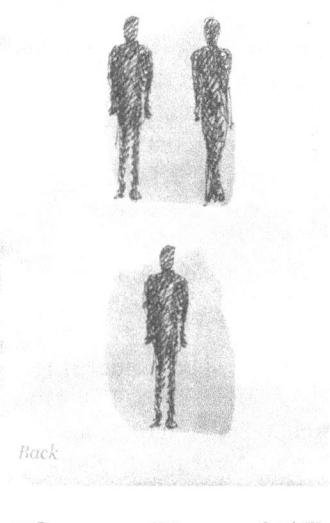

Choose an object that is different to your partner's choice.

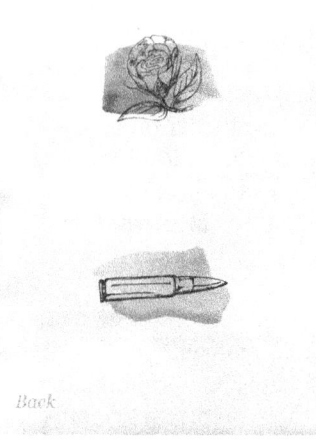

Figure 3.5 Screen grabs from the *Traces* app, which invites participants choose between a partner and an individual experience (top), and in the partner experience, to select difference routes through the narrative (bottom) (Credit: Hoffi/yello brick).

72   Traces: *A Case Study*

3   How is narrative accessed and experienced within immersive encounters? Is narrative cohesion desirable and practicable?
4   What happens when immersion 'fails'?

Our research design was thus oriented around exploring these questions with *Traces* participants, but without leading them and their responses so deliberately that other interesting or emergent themes would be missed. On first contact, we greeted participants and explained what would be expected of them; that they would first be 'doing' *Traces* and then meeting a researcher for a discussion afterwards.

On their return, they were invited to sit with the researcher and to start their exchange with a couple of activities. First, they were asked to map their *Traces* journey on paper:

> We would like you to spend the first five(ish) minutes visualizing/mapping your experience. You can base it on the physical journey you went on (as you remember it), or choose some other way of presenting it on the page (not necessarily drawing – could be eg a timeline). Be as creative as you like. Feel free to talk to me or to each other as you do this.
>
> [From *Traces* interview protocol]

This mapping activity was not designed to be a test of participants' recall of *Traces*, but instead to gain insights into what had been significant to them (if anything) during their journey on site, and to do so in a way that did not privilege their verbal responses. Sometimes participants took this as a prompt to draw a literal map of the route taken, but more often than that they foregrounded their interactions with the built and natural environment of St Fagans, as well as depicting how they had felt, and/or moments of friction in the piece. Figure 3.6 shows one example of these maps, and demonstrates well how people responded to this invitation. The 'map' centres on the participants' perceptions of – and encounters in – the built and natural environment without being a literal depiction of the site or of the journey. The many representations of archways here reflect their importance as threshold moments in the experience, framing the narrative and the landscape, and orienting the line of vision in *Traces*.

After drawing their map, participants were asked to describe what they had drawn and why they had drawn it, or to discuss and compare with their partner. Respondents were then tasked with summing up the *Traces* encounter in three words (as can also be seen depicted in Figure 3.6, in this case 'contemplative', 'soothing', and 'sensory') and verbally elaborating on their choice.

Figure 3.6 Sample participant mapping of *Traces* (Credit: image from project evaluation).

Only after these initial exercises did the discussion move into an exploration of the broader themes we were interested in for our research purposes. The remainder of the discussion was guided by a set of topics rather than an explicit and pre-ordered set of questions:

> OK, we've covered lots of really useful ground there, but if I can, I'd like to guide our discussion in some slightly different directions [start with those that have not been covered already]
>
> Interaction with the site [gardens, buildings, spaces]
> Felt experience of *Traces*
> The narrative
> *Traces* as immersive
> *Traces* as prompt
> Usability

In the following section, and with reference to the research questions outlined previously, we now briefly introduce the findings from those discussions, distilled from many hours of interview materials.[3] Here we begin to show how immersion was felt and experienced as itself a process of being and becoming, one that, despite its complexity, can be articulated usefully and powerfully within a research context.

74 Traces: *A Case Study*

Findings: Participant Perspectives on the Experience of Immersion

Previous research has highlighted the importance of framing and transitions to processes of audiencing and participation (Jackson 2011). The guiding principles, and even rules and permissions, that are (sometimes explicitly, but often more subtly) put in place for participants are incredibly important, yet can be tricky to navigate. In designing *Traces*, the team sought to build that framing into the experience itself in order to make it self-contained and easy for the site to maintain. The textual framing on the museum website and around the download on the app store was also used explicitly as a way of framing the experience and inducting those who would take part into a particular way of thinking about what they were about to do, and about the site:

> Traces is not an audio guide. Nor is it a tourist guide.
> It is a companion – telling you a story that reveals fragments of fact and fiction inspired by St Fagans; the space, its stories and archives.
> It is for the curious. For the seekers of mystery. And for those who are willing to get lost in the traces of a story.
> (National Museum Wales 2016)

Nevertheless, some participants[4] noted that they were puzzled by what to expect from Traces: *'I don't know what I expected'*, *'I'm just wondering whether it needs a little bit more information of what sort of experience it is before you do it, because I didn't know what it was going to be'* and:

> At the start, I wasn't quite sure what to expect. I knew it was going to be storytelling but I didn't know whether it was just going to be like a straight kind of audiobook guide or whether it was going to be someone's own story. So I felt intrigued there.

These feelings of puzzlement can be constructive and productive, especially where (as in the last example above) they also spark curiosity and intrigue. This was an unusual mode of heritage interpretation, so there were likely to be elements that participants felt unprepared for or were surprised by. Where these feelings spill into frustration, however, there is perhaps more to consider; were we doing enough to ensure participants were knowing and complicit agents within their experience? As has been noted previously (Kidd 2011, 2017), framing is especially important within heritage contexts where the stereotype of a prototypical 'visit' remains so strong and difficult to subvert. But framing is also difficult to do within sites that have physical restrictions; for example, given the fact this was an outdoor heritage attraction and a natural landscape, we were unable to add markers to promote the experience on site, or to reassure people that they were in the right place to start their journey. These kinds of restrictions are understandable perhaps, but we should be minded that they are also consequential in experiential terms.

One moment above all others was noted as key in transitioning into the narrative: Passing through the tunnel after the narrative introduction (on audio) and emerging on the castle side of the St Fagans site. Participants noted this as the point where they 'became' fully immersed in the storytelling and in the landscape. One participant reflected that *'going down to the tunnel was nice. I felt like you were descending into the labyrinth'* and another says *'It felt like a transition into another world, it really did, despite the fact we'd been here before and things like that'* continuing *'it felt like … we were entering an "other" space'*. It is interesting – and perhaps unsurprising – that a tunnel should be chosen by so many respondents as such an important threshold moment within the *Traces* encounter. Tunnels are key navigational and infrastructural devices within our everyday life and have structural significance, but also cultural, historical, and even political meanings. They help us overcome obstacles and provide literal and metaphorical access points to new (and familiar) terrains.

Respondents were quick to reflect on the ways in which their entanglement with the stories on offer through *Traces* was 'immersive'. 'Immersion' itself was a term we studiously avoided during the opening activities of our research interviews, but it was a term our participants often volunteered; as a sample of responses, one notes *'It was immersive throughout, I really felt I was retracing part of the story'* and another says *'the immersion was really there, I felt like I was part of it'*. Other lengthier quotes indicate the lines across which respondents' definitions of immersion were being drawn; as we had hoped it was the storytelling and its connections to the landscape rather than the technology that were key to the felt experience of immersion for most:

> it allows you to experience a familiar site in a completely different way. That immersion is really helpful with connecting

to certain stories, especially an emotional story as this one, with those deep sorts of feelings of longing and heartbreak and frustrated love and stuff like that. You can't communicate that easily in other ways, you've got to pull people into a narrative, pull people into a story, and it does that really well.

I think technology is at its best for something like this, when it's not all about everything that's on the screen and that it's more about the environment and this is just a tool for accessing it.

Other participants in the research did not use the term 'immersion', yet still talked in rich and dynamic ways about how they had become absorbed in the narrative world of *Traces*. One noted that '*It was like being inside a movie*' and another concludes that they '*just kind of shut off, and ... really got into the story and into the surroundings*'. To some of our participants, taking part in an immersive experience was itself a novelty, and a number noted that wearing headphones in particular was a new experience for them within the space of a heritage encounter. This nod to the hardware did not negatively impact on their experience; however, for the most part, it was as if the technology itself faded into the background (apart from where it was seen to 'fail' as discussed below). This has been noted previously as incredibly important to processes of immersion in digital cultural heritage projects (Kidd 2017). Indeed, the headphones seemed to be a way of focusing participants more on the natural environment and all it had to offer, an *'enhancement'*, rather than a silencing or muting of the landscape's power.

That the experience of immersion was such a positive one for our respondents meant that those moments when the experience jarred – for technical reasons for example – were all the more noticeable. Such moments appeared to break or frustrate respondents' capacity for immersion in the experience, although not irretrievably: '*The ways in which it didn't feel immersive I think were the sound balance issues with the app. The thing that took me out of the experience the most was that*'. Farman reflects on the consequences of 'technological breakdown' within (some) immersive experiences noting that 'When something breaks, that's when you notice it' (2015: 108). He observes that this is especially the case with mobile phones; these are technologies we use every day and that are woven into our lives in such ways as to be almost imperceptible until such time as they lose reception or battery life for example.

As is noted throughout this book, processes of participation are rarely straightforward, and responses to the invitation to make oneself visible through action can be mixed. This was seen to be the case in *Traces*. Most research respondents noted that *Traces* was a less 'passive' way of experiencing the site than they were used to, and commented on that as a very positive consequence of participation. They appreciated being asked to play, perform, and accomplish the small tasks: making a heart by positioning leaves, playing rock/paper/scissors, and leaving something in the space for example. One respondent details this beautifully:

> When I walked up to the kind of broken path and it's talking about Agnes skipping along beside you, jumping over the cracks, to the point where I stopped stepping on the cracks myself, kind of like joining in with the story. Rather than just listening to it, I wanted to do it as well, so I didn't step on the cracks.... People were looking at me like I was a weirdo with these headphones on and jumping over the cracks as an adult woman like, what is she doing, but I didn't care, I was kind of engrossed in the story.

For one or two others, however, the levels of interaction were out of kilter with what they were prepared to give in this encounter, as this quote demonstrates; '*I was a bit like I feel a bit silly doing that, and I don't feel silly doing many things*'. This demonstrates vividly the varied responses participants have to being implicated in the storytelling, even when there is actually little chance of their actions being noted or questioned by any 'observer' (this is for the most part a very quiet area of the St Fagans site, so chances were there were no observers around). Perhaps the response of this last participant actually nods to the difference between participation within what are ultimately quite narrow and bounded invitations to get involved (such as in *Traces*), and those that offer what might be understood as more genuine and uninhibited forms of agency.

Those that completed the partner experience all reflected that the social interactions fostered through that route were positive ones, and that their physical coming together and parting during *Traces* had been key to a constructive experience of immersion, as these respondents noted: '*I really liked the moments where it was clear that we were doing similar things but not quite and different instructions happened. I really liked those moments*' and '*knowing that someone has had a different narrative was beautiful,*

78 Traces: *A Case Study*

Figure 3.7 On the partner experience of *Olion,* the Welsh language equivalent of *Traces* (Credit: Alison John).

and not knowing what they may or may not do'. Moments where participants glimpse one another in a different part of the site, and encounter them as performers within the narrative, were particularly impactful, reminding us again that it is the storytelling itself upon which so much of the experience hangs: '*The image I had from that was really nice, to see you there as part of the story*' and another reflects '*Yes, I was on a bench on the other side. If you'd have turned around, you would have seen me. That was quite nice to see you sort of playing out the role that I was hearing.*'

Respondents talked vividly about how the landscape, the sensescape, and the soundscape (in and beyond the app) came together to provide a rich context for immersion. They enthused about the music, the lilt of the narration, the accent of the narrator, the smells of the site (real and imagined), touching and feeling a part of the built environment, and how they felt viscerally and (often) physiologically connected to the natural environment. Josephine Machon reflects on the importance of the (multi)sensory and the haptic in immersion when she says that 'awaking and engaging the fullness and diversity of sensory awareness is a central feature of immersive practice' (2013: 75) and continues 'haptic perception is a wholebody experience' which is 'often crucial' to immersion (2013: 77).

We see this very much in evidence in *Traces*, and people talk vividly and expansively about those processes:

> I felt like I was re-immersing myself in nature, which perhaps I wouldn't ordinarily do when I was here ... the scent of the wetness. So for me it was very tactile, my senses were heightened through the journey.

> 1: Yes, so when I was looking out of the gate and obviously it's basically winter and there are no plants out but when they mentioned the smell of lavender, I smelt lavender, so there was that sort of psychosomatic thing being brought out, which I thought was very powerful.
> 2: I pretty much said it was a pity that I couldn't smell the lavender because it's the wrong season and he was like, 'I smelt the lavender.'
> 1: I mean just for a second but it was definitely there

> 1: That's one of the things I think I'll take away, that moment when I had to walk along, running my fingers along the tree ...
> 2: The same when we were together, like putting our hands on that arch, that was really good.

Some reflected on these visceral and tactile moments as having a kind of transactional quality for and between themselves and the site; one where both emerged changed: '*Now I am a part of this place. I feel like I am more than just a visitor. It's quite powerful*'.

The above quotations from research discussions begin to demonstrate the ways in which people foregrounded talk about 'feeling' within this immersive encounter. Centring the self and affective response is to be expected within experiences that, as we have discussed in this book, are typified by their emphasis on participation, embodiment, and the sensorial and spatial qualities of interaction. The affective dimensions of *Traces* are not always easy for participants to articulate, however, and they sometimes find themselves moving through different patterns of engagement and emotional states. This emotional fluidity is universally experienced as a positive, leading to nuanced engagements with the site and its narratives, as another respondent reflected:

> Emotionally, I felt like there were parts that were quite poignant and made you think about war and loss and relationships

as an adult, and then there were other parts that really made you go straight back into childhood ... [I] kept on going back and forth between them.

Most respondents commented at some point that they have engaged emotionally with the narrative or with the experiential elements of *Traces*. In the majority of cases, people mirrored the narrative subject matter of *Traces* in their responses; they felt sad on occasion (parts of the narrative talk about loss, sadness, grief), but others found enjoyment and humour in it. Most equivocated between these two affective trajectories:

> The main bit that got me was the bit of the story there where you put your hands on the thing and you've got to think of happy memories and everything came flooding back to me, all these good memories I had and it was really nice. And there was sadness there when the mother died but she wore the crown of another's love, which was sweet and she'd leave the heart in leaves and they asked you to leave a penny.
>
> I felt happy, I felt sad and self-reflective but again, going back to the stones, I was like a kid again, and that kind of really innocent jumping on cracks, I didn't care what anyone was thinking, so that was a fun side of it as well. It was an array of emotions.

One of the aims of the *Traces* project was to impact, even if in small ways, how visitors navigate St Fagans. The castle side of the site is less often the focal point of a visit, and once there people often traverse it very quickly (often having left it to the end of a visit). *Traces* was designed to slow people down, to make them practice their visitation more thoughtfully, reflexively, and more intimately within the space of the castle and gardens. This was something respondents talked about a lot, many employing the currently expansive lexicon of 'wellbeing' to articulate their response to immersion. Amongst other terms used, we found Traces described as *'calming', 'relaxing', 'energising', 'serene', 'hypnotising', 'soothing', 'peaceful', 'dreamy', 'thoughtful', 'intimate', 'therapeutic', 'grounding', 'rejuvenating',* and *'a meditation'*. One partner discussion outlines this very nicely:

> 1: That bit at the end of close your eyes and taking you back into your memories, that was brilliant, that was really good because I don't know about you but I know I was standing

there with a really nice smile on my face, really enjoying that moment of coming back out of somebody else's story and back into your own.
2: That's what I put, it was really peaceful ... you kind of left on a bit of a high, didn't you?

Respondents noted that it felt like an *'escape'* or *'escapism'*, again nodding to the sense that this is an atypical form of museum visiting, facilitated through practices of immersion. But such sentiments perhaps also related to the form of the story. Traces is a linear narrative in that it has a clear beginning, middle, and end, but it is characterised throughout by fragmentation. It is perhaps better described as a series of vignettes about people, place, and the landscape. This fragmentation was again for the most part experienced as a positive: *'I thought it was quite disjointed, to be honest ... [but] it didn't really matter. It didn't follow an A to B'* noted one respondent, and another reflected that *'although it wasn't extremely structured in how it kind of developed because I felt like that was a good thing because it kind of let you make your own thoughts'*. However, there were times where the fractured narrative appears to have frustrated people; some want to know more about these characters and their stories and find that thirst unquenched (as Alke notes in her analysis in the opening section of this chapter). One respondent reflects that the narrative is *'nearly like an archaeological dig'*, an insightful description directly in keeping with what we were trying to achieve with *Traces*. The story (or stories) in the app is informed by and consumed within the landscape of St Fagans, and that gives them a particular kind of narrative power, as McErlean notes, 'context influences the interpretation of narrative texts' (McErlean 2018: 45). But as McErlean goes on to point out, context can be multiply defined and identified, meaning interpretations are ultimately subjective and 'cannot be accurately foreseen' (McErlean 2018: 62). It is exactly this subjectivity that makes research with participants endlessly insightful, rewarding, and fascinating. They paint a rich picture of the processes, felt experiences, and limitations of immersion which is instructive for future practice.

Orientation: Story

Having systematically and empirically explored the orientations of creation, process, and participant, we now focus on how story emerges at the intersections of these orientations, and reflect on

82   Traces: *A Case Study*

whether – and to what extent – *Traces* might be considered an immersive story as a result. We will then also briefly consider *Traces* as part of the larger context of the St Fagans site and discuss whether this adds up to what could be considered a cohesive storyworld.

Approach and Methods

The intersectionality of the story orientation means that in order to arrive at an analysis of it, we need to consider what happens in the other orientations. In short, the approach is one of triangulation. It is with the help of these different perspectives that we can identify the ambitions, but also the practical limitations of a storytelling experience, and its potential for immersion.

Findings

As has already been shown, the story orientation of *Traces* is complicated, because while there is a narrative, it is presented in fragments – the traces of the title. The participant becomes an observer, explorer, and witness to these fragments, but has to do much of the work of piecing them together (solving the puzzle) on their own, or retrospectively with their partner. However, these fragments do have a dramatic dimension: they tell of love, loss, and recuperation, and it emerged in many of the participant interviews that the approach had engaged participants' imaginations very deeply. This was not the case for everybody however, and some participants found this fragmentation a barrier to conceptual immersion in the storyworld that was being presented.

Although fragmented, the experience itself is a linear one, meaning that participants have little agency over the ordering of their journey, or the aspects of it they encounter, beyond their capacity to skip sections, or to switch off and walk away if they wish. As has been noted, this linearity was in large part a consequence of limitations imposed by the technical infrastructure of the St Fagans site, rather than the ambitions of the creators. That said, it is not clear that a more complex narrative structure would have lessened barriers to immersion rather than increased them.

As is revealed in the ways research participants articulated their responses to *Traces*, the most compelling way in which this storytelling experience can be considered immersive is in the ways the audio format and the direction of the narrator foregrounds focused looking and subtly encourages different kinds of visitor performances on site: slower, more intentional, and more affectively attuned. The many ways the narrative references and seamlessly integrates the features of the castle gardens that the experience is set in – both spatial and sensory (which we explored as part of the creation orientation) – were cited as compelling pathways to immersion for all of our participants bar none. The simplicity of this in technical terms is interesting to note. Immersion here is not dependent on removing real-world stimuli (far from it), or on a sense of complete 'presence' within a virtual encounter, but instead is a consequence of multimodality, simple interaction, and deep affective engagement in a found space.

Traces is located within the larger context of St Fagans and could be understood as part of the larger storyworld created in and around that site (Kidd 2018b). In many ways, it is a sympathetic form of interpretation, in that the site itself is one constituted of fragments, not least in the form of the more than 40 buildings that have been (and continue to be) translocated from all over Wales. These buildings include iron age roundhouses, nineteenth-century mills, a row of cottages (each one furnished according to a different era from 1800 to 1985), a series of workshops, a general store and bakehouse, a pigsty, an air raid shelter, a 'House of the Future,' and a pub. St Fagans is then already an assemblage of fragments, a storyworld that can be accessed in various conditions of completion, one that contains conflicting truths that will not be reconciled, and one which has the capacity to surprise at every corner. *Traces* is set apart from this because it explores an area that is original to the location – the castle and the gardens were here before this became a museum. However, in developing the fragmented approach to its story, it in a way mimics what is going on in the rest of the site, whilst using audio as a delivery method. Perhaps then, the *Traces* experience is immersive in a different way than the rest of the St Fagans storyworld, while still tying into its overall narrative, that of telling the story of Wales through fragments.

Summary

In this chapter, we have used one immersive storytelling encounter – *Traces* – as a lens through which to explore the characteristics of immersive storytelling. We have explored the textual experience of *Traces*, offering a detailed overview and analysis of how it works in practice: thematically, spatially, sensorially, temporally, and transmedially. We then provided an insight into how it was created, introducing *Traces* as a creative process, working with clear ambitions, but limited by practical considerations. Third, we introduced research into the lived and felt experience of participation in *Traces*. Last, we explored the intersection of these three orientations by focusing on the story and its immersiveness. *Traces* is designed – and promoted – with deep immersion in mind. It is intended that it will forge new connections between people, and between people and place. We have begun to explore the degree to which those ambitions have been met in *Traces*, yet in doing so, have made visible the complexities of immersive experience, rather than resolve or smooth them over. Experiences of immersion emerge in *Traces* as uniquely situated, but with resonances that we can talk across as 'findings'.

By using the Layers of Experience framework as a starting point for our analysis, we have demonstrated a way to systematically explore all of these elements. Our approach here is not the only way that we could have done this however. We could have carried out and included more precise mapping of the space and how people navigated it, in-depth interviews with other members of the creative team, or questionnaires with a larger number of participants. We could also have introduced a comparative analysis of similar experiences, within or beyond other heritage settings. Researching experiences is complex (Gröppel-Wegener 2011; Galani and Kidd 2019), but we have demonstrated here that it is by no means a hopeless endeavour. Immersive stories and storyworlds breathe in dynamic and sometimes ungovernable ways, creations are complex, creators' ambitions are often hidden, and participant responses are often unpredictable. This is what makes them such fascinating objects of study.

Notes

1 We have had unique access to *Traces* whilst writing this book as Jenny was one of the project partners, and we are therefore able to analyse it fully from a number of perspectives.
2 Unusually for multilanguage versions, these were not translations of each other, but rather two independently written stories, albeit by the same writer and covering the same material.
3 Further analysis of the more expansive data has been published as Huws et al. (2019).
4 Participants' comments are being shown in italics.

4 Against Immersion?

This book has centred encounters in immersion, both our own and other people's. We have sought to reconcile the experience of *being* immersed, and the challenges of researching in immersive contexts, with the ways in which immersion is structured, activated, and promoted in the pursuit of story. Yet, those processes are not neutral, raising ethical and philosophical questions as we have noted. This chapter foregrounds those questions in a reminder that it is criticality itself that we wish to promote as a practice of reflexivity in and around immersive encounters.

The critiques we present in this chapter are a feature of debates about immersive media and interactive storytelling more broadly, and most authors writing on these themes touch on them at least in passing. But they are rarely aggregated as a series of charges *against* immersion as they are here. We think this overview is useful because such critiques have been intensifying, demanding both recognition and response.

There are four 'charges' against immersion presented in this chapter, with reference to literature and examples to help elucidate the themes. Firstly, we review critiques of immersive practice that circulate around questions of power in participation. These challenge the view that audience- or user-centred experiences *necessarily* offer more (and more dynamic forms of) agency, and that they are more empowering as a result. In the second charge, we introduce criticisms of the ways in which immersive experiences are being 'co-opted' by mainstream consumer culture, using literature on the experience economy and aesthetic capitalism. Our third charge is one that mostly relates to the digital – video gaming in particular – and this is that immersion fosters engagement and escapism to a degree that can become problematic (even addictive), and that it therefore needs to be approached with caution. Fourthly, and relatedly, we explore how discourses about immersion can be characterised as technocratic. Even though we have not in this book worked with a definition of immersion that prioritises digitality, we have noted that 'thinking digitally' is often a feature of this landscape (Causey 2016). Here we ask what the implications of that perspective are, and why it might be considered problematic.

These four charges are interwoven in complex ways, but we do our best to unpack them here in an accessible manner. Because of this connectedness, however, we have decided to state them first separately, before responding to them as a whole to offer some counterarguments. This approach mirrors that of previous chapters. As has been shown, it can be easier to approach these complex subjects by prising the layers apart, but at the end of the day, judging them holistically. We end the chapter with some brief concluding remarks.

During discussions at the start of our writing project, we remained ambivalent about whether these critiques were so urgent as to necessitate inclusion in what was always intended to be a short book. We disagreed about the extent to which they retained their potency in a landscape where the practice we were encountering had become so often itself reflexive on these themes.[1] Many immersive theatre projects for example now foreground questions of power, technocracy, and social justice (such as National Theatre Wales and The Space's *Bordergame* 2014, Blast Theory and Hydrocracker's *Operation Black Antler* 2017, yello brick's *Extinct* 2018, Dotdotdot's *Somnai* 2018), and other works are making concerted attempts to increase the visibility of voices and experiences previously marginalised. Derek Ham's Virtual Reality (VR) storytelling project *I Am a Man*, for example, centres the experiences of those who fought for equality as part of the African-American Civil Rights Movement, and Nonny de la Peña's *Hunger in Los Angeles* simulates (again in VR) the experience of watching a man go into diabetic shock at a Los Angeles food bank in order to raise awareness about poverty and its impacts. There are a number of immersive journalism initiatives that are attempting to connect audiences more viscerally and intentionally with the news agenda (for more examples see Carson 2015).

Such projects can be considered reassuring as ripostes to the critiques presented in this chapter, and they attest to the positive potential of the field(s) of immersive storytelling to respond to the challenge posed by Lukas in the following quotation:

> Is it possible to use critical awareness of the issues and problems associated with immersion ... in order to fashion new

Against Immersion? 87

spaces, modalities, and understandings of immersion that are more critical, conceptual, even political?

(Lukas 2016: 118)

Such practice notwithstanding however, we (as authors) have both continued to find ourselves on occasion staggered by a lack of framing in (some) immersive experiences, or as confused and irritated by what those experiences were asking us to give, instances that required us to offer up our own stories and closely guarded secrets, our emotional responses, our empathy, our personal space, or our data, for what seemed inexplicable or indefensible ends. We have noted that much of the marketing literature about the creation of 'storyworlds' continues to advocate for the *exploitation* of emotion with little regard to the ethical dimensions of that practice (for example McStay 2016), and we continue to find the technology being too regularly and simplistically conflated with immersion itself (particularly the case with VR, AR, and XR in 2018). These shortcomings in the discursive field of immersive storytelling, especially as they translate into mainstream discourse, have often made us uneasy.

It would seem then that these critiques do bear revisiting.

Charge 1: Immersion ≠ Power

Debates about power dynamics within participatory, interactive, and immersive contexts are complex and (now) extensive. Within performance studies, scholarly debates about experimentation with form and content have been ongoing since the 1960s (Schechner 1973; Lorek-Jezinska 2002), and 'frame-breaking' (Bennett 1990: 153) is now a regular feature of immersive theatre practice in particular. Across media and cultural institutions, we have seen increased interest in crowdsourcing, co-curation and co-production, or in social media and video sharing sites like YouTube as a means of levelling the playing field, and opening up access. The *potentials* of interaction have often been heralded as paradigm shifting, as in some way inherently democratising and empowering. Increased participation has been promoted as a means of diversifying narratives, engaging communities, and flattening hierarchies of knowledge production and acquisition. Participation is framed as in some way morally 'good' in comparison to hierarchical patterns of influence that (are understood to) inspire only apathy and passivity. Yet, those claims may have been short lived given that, according to Adam

Fish, 'the trendiness of the term "democratization" peaked in 2005' (2017: 1). It is now broadly recognised that the impacts of participation are more equivocal, as was highlighted so startlingly during the Facebook and Cambridge Analytica scandal in 2018.

As we foreground the participatory aspect as crucial to immersive experiences, it is useful to be reminded that the notion of 'participation' in culture emerged in the realm of the political – in community arts, development studies, and fan communities – where it was allied to notions of democracy. Yet, in recent years, it has been co-opted in the realm of the commercial and the mainstream where it has itself become a form of spectacle (Bishop 2012). Henry Jenkins, Sam Ford, and Joshua Green for example, have criticised how mainstream media producers have appropriated practices as 'user-generated content' and 'branded platforms' (Jenkins et al. 2013: xi) in unimaginative and exploitative ways.

Critiques of participation and its rhetorics have been burgeoning across Arts, Humanities, and Social Sciences disciplines. In his thoughtful book on *The Sharing Economy*, Arun Sundararajan unpicks and unsettles the idea that power is being reoriented by and towards 'the "crowd"' (2017: 2), outlining the ways in which the logics of the sharing economy can be understood as exploitative. Nico Carpentier reviewed the political and ideological underpinnings of the use of the term 'participation' in 2011, and in 2013 Sonia Livingstone presented a detailed and provocative critique of what she termed the 'participation paradigm'. To both Livingstone and Carpentier, participation is indelibly and problematically ensnared with questions about power, and they demonstrate how a straightforward shift from a lexicon of passivity to one that foregrounds agency is one that ignores the decades of literature problematising that binary within Media and Cultural Studies (and we would also add Museum and Heritage Studies, Cultural Policy Studies, and Development Studies for example).

It is notable, however, that despite the above critiques certain domains continue to privilege talk about the agentic potentials of immersion: activating and repeating particular kinds of discursive formulations (Foucault 1979, 1981). This is particularly true of the marketing and promotions discourse that circulates around events, hardware, platforms, or installations that are 'immersive'; for example, the Oculus Go is sold on a promise that it will enable users to 'take control of every adventure' and the Google Cultural Institute promotes it's ***Museum View*** functionality by proposing that it 'transcends physical boundaries', giving users 'exclusive access' to sites. In this book, we have perhaps compounded that problem to some degree in our own centring of the user–audience–interactant–participant and their 'experience' within our definition of the core characteristics of immersion. Yet, we demonstrated how problematic the concept of participation is in Chapter 3 where we looked at how participants themselves talked about their own experiences of immersion. Bill Cooke and Uma Kothari have powerfully written about participation as a new and misunderstood 'tyranny' (2001: 3). Might immersive storytelling too be understood as tyrannical?

Claire Bishop challenges the centrality of notions of participation within collaborative arts programmes arguing that the benefits of participation are ill-understood and over-articulated (Bishop 2012; see also Freshwater 2009). She goes further to assert that illusions of agency within participatory environments can actually serve to *dis*empower those who take part (Bishop 2012). There is nothing more disempowering than to labour under the illusion that you have agency, only to discover that it is tokenistic, can be rescinded or disallowed. We have noted in this book how difficult 'experiences' are to measure and articulate, and this of course compounds the problem, to the point where Mosse calls participation an 'act of faith' (Mosse 2001). Do we really understand how processes of participation differ from more typical forms of spectatorship – listening, gazing, or stillness for example? (Rancière 2009). And do we understand the circumstances under which an invitation to participate within an immersive context might be rejected? Josephine Machon notes that there 'is often a "love it or loathe it"' response to immersive theatre (2013: 41), and others have used extensive longitudinal research with participants in heritage performances to consolidate a case for the importance of 'framing' and 'induction' in those encounters, particularly in contexts where an immersive experience might be unanticipated (Kidd 2011). This has been important in working towards more nuanced ways of framing immersive encounters, but as we noted in Chapter 3, these do not work for everybody. As Machon concludes, 'a large number of individuals dislike this type of practice' (2013: 41) and it follows that 'the immersive form requires care in its execution'. Securing the kinds of investment – physical, emotional, sensorial, cognitive – that immersive work often benefits from is not straightforward. Mangen and van der Weel, in their study of the limits of web storytelling, conclude that 'it appears that the hierarchical relationship between the author and a receptive, passive reader, despised by hypertext theoreticians, is really exactly what the reader of narrative fiction wants and expects' (2017: 175). John Bucher points out that people's tolerance for immersive experiences may well be limited, reminding us that theme parks continue to build in 'passive attractions' like shows that mean visitors can 'escape the immersion' and its requirements when they feel the need to (Bucher 2017: 83). To go back to our analogy of liquid immersion from the opening chapter, not everybody finds the thought of an open water dive appealing – or appealing all of the time – even though its potential to thrill and release adrenaline might be evident.

The above concerns about participation in part circulate around perceptions of risk in that 'there is a sense of putting oneself on the line, often in the presence of others' (Alston 2013: 134). Alston goes on to detail this notion of risk at some length:

> There is first of all the risk of not understanding the protocols of a given theatrical practice; there is also the risk of participatory rules being unclear … I would add that the taking of participatory risks also relates to the production of affect and emotion. Embarrassment, awkwardness, guilt and shame become potential risks for participating audiences.
> (Alston 2013: 134)

This intersects with debates in the next section about neo-liberalism where risk is similarly a potent part of the discourse. Using the work of Punchdrunk – and in particular *The Masque of the Red Death* – Alston explores the kind of audiencing produced in immersive theatre as a form of 'entrepreneurial participation' which rewards those who are willing to take the most risks, to the extent that 'participatory opportunity is often unevenly [and inequitably] distributed' (Alston 2013: 133). This exposes the claims to democracy and empowerment recounted earlier as partial at best; new ways of articulating and performing one's cultural capital (Bourdieu 1997) begin to emerge in immersive formats. Certain kinds of responses to immersion can become learned, practiced, and in time, sedimented.

Charge 2: Immersion Has Been Co-opted by the Mainstream

> There is a bandwagon being jumped on that is exploiting an increasing desire amongst non-mainstream theatre audiences to delve into a reality that both replaces and accentuates the

live(d) existence of the everyday, actual world. As the term and elements of the form are appropriated and overused in this way, then there is a subsequent push into, and appropriation by, the mainstream.

(Machon 2013: 60–61)

Josephine Machon's 2013 case that the rise in encounters defined or promoted as 'immersive' represents an 'appropriation' of the form is provocative and strongly argued. Going as far as to suggest that 'there is a bandwagon being jumped on' and that audiences are being 'exploited', Machon implies that a cynical 'overuse' of the term is emptying it of meaning. In a similar vein, Alston argues that 'immersive theatre is particularly susceptible to co-optation by a neoliberal market given its compatibility with the growing experience industry' (Alston 2013: 128), and proposes that as a result 'supposedly tailor-made experiences are churned out for a production line of participating cultural consumers' (Alston 2013: 131).

Both Machon and Alston are activating another set of critiques here that pivot on the relationship between immersive practice and what has been called 'the experience economy' (Pine and Gilmore 1998). This proposes that the capacity – and will – to purchase experiences has 'emerged as the next step in ... the progression of economic value', so a shift from the consumption of goods, to the consumption of services, to now, the consumption of experiences (Pine and Gilmore 1998). To Pine and Gilmore, 'an experience occurs when a company intentionally uses services as the stage, and goods as props, to engage individual customers in a way that creates a memorable event' (Gilmore 1998). Such experiences are important within the entertainment business but, according to Pine and Gilmore's thesis, are increasingly significant for other businesses also; whether you are selling flights or cups of coffee, making an experience of consumption 'memorable' has a direct impact on its profitability. The marketing industry in particular has been keen to move into this space, seeing the kinds of 'experience' that can be fostered through alternate reality gaming and transmedia storytelling (for example) as highly seductive and lucrative.

One case study of immersive storytelling that demonstrates well this notion of the experience economy is *Secret Cinema*. Since 2007, the company has been creating immersive cinema experiences: **'360-degree participatory Secret Worlds** where the boundaries between performer and audience, set and reality are constantly shifting.' (Secret Cinema undated, original emphasis). A *Secret*

Cinema experience is not about seeing a new film release; it is the experience itself that is being paid for. Often the films selected are considered cult and already have an established fan base, for example the first ***Secret Cinema*** production of 2018 was centred around the film *Blade Runner*, originally released in 1982. One could argue that these events are not about the screenings at all, but rather about allowing the audience to become part of a much-loved movie themselves, in the case of 'Secret Cinema presents: Blade Runner: The Final Cut: A Secret Live Experience' to enter the dystopian future and enjoy some noodles amongst the high rises and alleyways drenched in neon lights. These secret worlds are expansive and much anticipated by their fan base, meaning that ***Secret Cinema*** has now secured themselves an unrivalled position in the market for cinematic experiences. Participants are willing to pay far more for a ticket to a ***Secret Cinema*** screening than they would for a regular cinema visit.

Some scholars are agitated by the ways in which immersive practice has been aligned with, and subsumed within, the experience economy, especially as it elides with marketing and advertising. As noted above, the lexicon used is often hostile; this is practice that is being 'co-opted' and 'appropriated' in ways that are deemed unhelpful at best, and cynical at worst. As Matthew Reason reminds us however, this term 'experience' has itself in time become an accepted part of the promotions packages through which numerous immersive encounters and storyworlds are packaged and sold to us (2015: 272). Referencing Rancière's *Emancipated Spectator* (2009), Reason questions whether such practices might be best understood as forms of 'consumerist hyper-activism' that engulf us and stifle our criticality (2015: 274). Claire Bishop asserts that participation rather than being oppositional to spectacle is now 'entirely merged with it' (2012: 277), undermining the claims to sociopolitical impact that might typically be made in its name, and instead enlivening it to commercial interests, as with other forms of spectacle (Debord 1967). Nicola Shaughnessy notes that those who create immersive practice can anticipate charges that it is an 'artificial, manufactured, consumerist product, reducing art to a series of cheap (or expensive) simulated thrills' (2012: 186). In these arguments, immersive experiences lose something of their potency and radicality by dint of their absorption into a consumerist agenda. These criticisms then centre seemingly problematic connections between 'experience' and consumption, the 'corporatization of leisure' to use a phrase from Hayles et al. (2014: 221). Here we find ourselves at the antithesis of

Against Immersion? 93

the discourse about agency and democratisation problematised in the previous section.

Peter Murphy and Eduardo de la Fuente's 2014 book *Aesthetic Capitalism* gives us a lens and a language to review connections between visual culture and contemporary economic processes. In their thesis art, creativity, images, marketing, and experience are all in danger of being understood as little more than ways of producing economic value, and particularly effective ones at that, as Murphy proposes, 'the modern corporation either mutates into the art firm or else it goes bankrupt' (2014: 62). Hutter queries whether 'the ever expanding capitalist perspective' might in fact be 'internalizing the arts and the surrounding fields of aesthetic practice?' (2016: 128) and Böhme (2017) notes how this filters down to an individual level where the 'staging' of one's life becomes an aesthetic project; think for example of the contents of Instagram, Pinterest, and *Wired* magazine. Being seen to consume immersive experiences becomes a part of that staging, and we take our place within what has become, according to Böhme, a 'performance society' (2017, see also Goffman 1956). Increased attention to aesthetics, design, and experience is mirrored in the prevalence of discourse about 'the creative industries' and (more recently) 'the creative economy', which have emerged from governmental policy frameworks and rhetoric, and resulted in the contributions of core creative sectors[2] being assessed in instrumental – and predominantly economic – terms. Much of the activity we have looked at in this book would sit firmly within the domain of the creative industries, and, depending on its funding arrangements, may be tasked with final project reporting within quite narrow parameters for success (and failure).

It is easy to understand the appeal of (for example) experiential marketing to those who have something to sell. As McErlean notes, the historic spend on marketing through established channels (that is, around the 'consumption of traditional media' like radio, television, and newspapers) is likely to be eclipsed given the 'commercial potential of individually identifiable interactive engagements with story elements' (McErlean 2018: 10), especially in what has become an incredibly hostile climate for 'traditional' advertising. When marketing and promotions can be personalised, multi-sensorial, affectively attuned, and environmentally aware, it is a seductive logic to imagine that they might be more impactful. It is not surprising then that advertisers have made inroads into this space. Many product launches themselves are now framed as experiences; Apple are famous for their much-anticipated launch events, and car companies such as Mercedes-Benz have followed suit, crafting experiences that are designed to be captured and shared through networks via mobile phone footage. See for example the launch of the Mercedes-AMG GT in Shanghai 2015. The short film covering the event, available on YouTube, is a classic demonstration of how the logics of 'experience' are being utilised as a pathway to audiences far beyond those who might be present in the room at the time. Featuring not only the cars, but a slick series of 3D projections, flashing lights, and music, attendees arrive and navigate their way through a series of projections to their seats. Thereafter they can be seen with phones in hand, capturing the event to be shared via social media.

These are extensions of the 'immersive' that make many theorists and practitioners uneasy. Do they distort the field for those who are interested in subtler, edgier, and less slick productions? What about 'brands' that emerge from a storyworld? In Chapter 2 we introduced a range of examples from the *Harry Potter* storyworld, a world that started as a simple story but has since developed into a phenomenon that undoubtedly has an economic and capitalist dimension. Are immersive experiences and storyworlds somehow less meaningful once they have entered that space? Immersive storytelling is a complex and mixed-media economy that continues to resist simple distinctions and classification.

Charge 3: Immersion Fosters Addiction

Taking on a different life, whether by stepping into an established character (as we have seen in the case of the *Harry Potter* video games referred to in Chapter 2), or creating your own via an avatar – even creating and playing multiple characters – demonstrates how digitally immersive experiences can be ready-made opportunities for escapism. The best immersive experiences, the ones where participants' emotional buy-in (or presence) is highest, are those that don't just build a believable environment, but also foster high levels of engagement within it (indeed, the Experience Economy model describes the escapism sector as the one that requires both active participation and immersion, Pine and Gilmore 1998; also see Qu 2017). With high levels of engagement, however, comes (seemingly) the potential for addiction, to the extent that 'gaming disorder' was proposed as a behavioural condition by the World Health Organization in 2018. This has been a contentious proposal (Therrien 2018), but it demonstrates well some of the anxieties that emerge in this particular 'charge'.

Of course, it is not the case that every exposure to immersive experiences leads to addiction. This has mainly been researched in the context of video gaming and has been found to be in no way straightforward (Deleuze et al. 2018; Triberti et al. 2018); such addictions emerge at the intersection of a number of different phenomena. Seah and Cairns in their exploration 'From Immersion to Addiction in Videogames' (2008) state that 'engagement is hard to distinguish from addictive behaviours around playing videogames. Immersion, the actual experience of playing, does relate to engagement and may be a factor leading to addiction in videogames' (Seah and Cairns 2008: 1). They attempt to measure immersion by looking at both game factors, such as the challenge a game provides to its players and the control and agency provided by the game to its players, and psychological factors, 'specifically the cognitive and emotional involvement in the game and the sense of dissociation from the real world' (Seah and Cairns 2008: 2).

> It might be that because of player disposition to be highly engaged with videogames, the playing experience is more intensely immersive or that, because of more immersive playing experience, the player is more likely to become highly engaged. In practice, it seems likely to be a mix of the two with rewarding immersive experiences leading to better engagement and increased desire to play and longer playing times leading to an increased sense of immersion – being lost for longer in the game.
>
> (Seah and Cairns 2008: 7)

Connectedly, it has been found that whether intense gaming develops into something akin to addiction is not necessarily a matter of the game itself, but rather of the personality of the player. Specifically, Loton et al. (2016) found a link that suggests that people who tend to avoid their problems in the real world, rather than try to solve them, are more likely to use a video game as a method of avoidance, which can foster higher engagement and lead to addictive behaviour.[3]

The genre of the video game seems particularly open to scrutiny with regard to debates about addiction, not least because players have a lot of agency over how much and how long they engage – theoretically this could be 24 hours a day. Very few other storytelling genres afford this level of access; you are not limited by the run time of a play or film or opening and closing times of a theme park, for example. In addition, the video game and related genres often come with the potential for both visual and auditory immersion via headsets, allowing players to literally drown out the outside world. This is not to say that other storytelling genres do not also provide the opportunity for escapism. In fact, it could be argued that theme parks, as conceived by Walt Disney, started out with exactly that purpose. Karal Ann Marling argues that Disney

> did not believe for a moment that art – his art, the picture-postcard kind – was obliged to be disturbing, challenging, unsettling. He believed instead that it ought to provide refuge from that world of woes he knew at first hand. His park was built behind a berm to protect it from the evils that daily best humankind on all sides. It aimed to soothe and reassure. It aimed to give pleasure. Joy. A flash of sunny happiness. The small, sweet, ordinary, domestic emotions seldom implicit in the definition of aesthetic pleasure. The architecture of reassurance.
>
> (Marling 1997: 83)

These places are ideal to escape from life for an afternoon or indeed a holiday. But although there is anecdotal evidence that some people consider themselves 'addicted' to theme parks (see for example Frost 2017), this seems to be used almost as a badge of honour amongst fans, rather than seen as problematic. And of course, at some point you will need to leave the theme park, and even if you extend the experience further by staying in an attached resort hotel, unless you have considerable funds, you will need to go home and back to the real world at some point.

That doesn't mean that we cannot see these places, as well as storyworlds that encompass a multitude of genres, as experiences that foster the types of high engagement that are explored in the video game scholarship. Seeking out different ways a story extends across genres can be an escape from everyday life, and merchandise in particular can allow a storyworld to leak into this everyday life. Whether this is harmless fun or obsessive escapism (and/or excessive commodity fetishism, Marx 1867) is a matter of degrees, but it shows the potentially seductive power of immersive stories and storyworlds yet again.

It seems like the escapist aspects of immersive storytelling experiences are what opens the door to possibly addictive behaviours, but that this is by no means a common phenomenon, or a straightforward process. As we have seen, it is more likely to be observed in relation to genres that provide high levels of psychological and physiological immersion and engagement, and it would seem that some people are more predisposed than others to let experiences escalate in this way. What is interesting to note here also is how inflammatory public debate around these issues has become. Within the media, in particular, there is something of a moral panic playing out in relation to those who game, which bleeds into associated debates about (for example) how much screen time is acceptable for children. Such reporting heavily relies on stereotypes of gamers and problematic assertions about links between game play and (say) increased proclivity for violent actions or problems with socialising. Focusing solely on the supposed addictive qualities of games plays into attempts to 'pathologize' them (Bean et al. 2017) in ways that would seem curious for other formats (book reading for example). It is then in notions of immersion, presence, and experience that those accusations find their footing.

Charge 4: The Discourse about Immersion Is Technocratic

As noted, we have been careful in this book not to foreground the technological in our definitions and appraisals of immersive storytelling. Yet, there is no question that much immersive storytelling practice does rely on digital hardware and platforms, mixed-reality environments, and/or intersections of the digital and analogue. This much was apparent in the previous section. Acknowledging that, however, is not the same as saying that immersive stories are a digital phenomenon. Readers of this book will hopefully be aware of that nuance, but it is not uncommon in our experience to encounter perspectives that privilege immersive technologies to the exclusion of all else; for example, the viewpoint that immersive storytelling is necessarily going to involve some manner of VR and/or Augmented Reality (AR). Such perspectives make us uneasy because privileging the technological rather than (say) the humanistic is unlikely to lead us to jointly *ethical* and *enriching* immersive encounters with story. Humanistic approaches are crucial as they foreground 'questions of conscience and obligation, of recognition and respect, of justice and law' (Peter Dews 2002 quoted in Bishop 2012: 25) that can become lost in purely technocratic systems (that is, those that centre science and technology, particularly for systems of control).

In the first section of this chapter, we reviewed debates about whether participatory and immersive media could be understood as inherently democratic. These claims have especially accompanied developments in digital technology over the last 30 years; the invention of the World Wide Web in 1989, the launch of Facebook in 2004, and YouTube in 2005, and the launch of the small and inexpensive single-board computer Raspberry Pi in 2012 for example. As Evgeny Morozov provocatively proposed in 2011, 'the only place where the West ... is still unabashedly eager to promote democracy is in cyberspace' (2011: xii). But claims about the democratising potentials of technologies are not new. They have accompanied technological change through time, for example, the invention of the printing press was (and remains) heralded for its potentials as a tool for democracy, and for progress. What we often encounter in these claims is a sense that the technology itself will affect (positive) change – technological utopianism coupled with a deep-seated technological determinism.[4] Yet, we must remember that technologies are invented and shaped by humans, and that humans are multiply conditioned and biased. That the debate about immersion sits so neatly alongside developments in technology should therefore give us pause for thought. This section details a number of challenges for thinking through different points of intersection between immersion and technology.

Digital media are often (mis)understood as immaterial, and our interactions with them are (mis)characterised as not physically grounded. These perspectives need challenging. Seeing digital as immaterial neglects 'the material conditions that make possible the computing practice[s] that exist around the world' and associated environmental issues that come about due to our increased reliance on technology (Farman 2015: 103). Server farms, mineral mining, and huge production lines are a reality of the tech industry, and electronic waste – whether hardware or detritus left in the cloud – has a tangible quality and is a by-product of our interactions with the digital. In addition, seeing digital media as weightless and immaterial ignores the fact that for many people their use can be physically challenging and even alienating; human–computer interactions can be clunky and unwieldy, far from frictionless or (the ideal) invisible. Access issues are still a major problem, and digital divides along a number of trajectories are still a major barrier to participation for many, persisting along the lines of geography, class, ethnicity, gender, and ability, for example (Reed 2014). Questions of access remind us that digital encounters are grounded

Against Immersion? 99

in real-world contexts and are far from disembodied (Reed 2014).[5] We would argue that issues of sustainability and accessibility need to be more visible within debates at the points where immersion intersects with the digital.

When we introduced charges that immersive media might be considered agents of neo-liberalism in a previous section, we stopped short of introducing discussion about technoliberalism that seemed more appropriate to review here. Nick Srnicek highlights the sedimented interrelationship between capitalist systems and technology when he notes that 'capitalism … demands constant technological change' (2017: 12) and Adam Fish (2017) presents a troubling account of the structures that underpin and legitimise certain ways of using technologies over others in his book on *Technoliberalism*. Whilst acknowledging that technologies *can* animate political action and democracy, Fish's account details how control over technological innovation largely resides with 'major corporate forces' (2017: 3) and provocatively asserts even in the title of his book that we might be seeing the end of participatory culture. Digital platforms are not neutral or benign. As David Spencer notes, digital technologies are 'themselves products of unequal power – they are not neutral as such, but rather are created, harnessed and reproduced under conditions where power resides with capital, not labour' (2017: 142). In addition, their origins (often within start-ups with Silicon Valley mentalities) mean that individualism and the free market structure the kinds of technological developments that are prioritised, as well as indicating which will be de-prioritised. These inevitably reflect the needs and desires of a limited demography with a limited world view.

Concurrently, we find that 'capitalism has turned to data' (Srnicek 2017: 6), 'a massive new raw material to appropriate' (ibid: 88). In recent years, we have begun to understand more about the damaging consequences of rampant technoliberalism and the almost unchecked collation (and sale) of data, how it impinges on our liberties, and even interferes with our democratic processes (Greenfield 2018). Joanna Redden and Jessica Brand (2017) have compiled a record of 'data harms' which catalogues some of the most pernicious extensions of what has been termed 'surveillance capitalism' (Zuboff 2017; Turner 2018) and 'surveillance realism' (Dencik and Cable 2017).

But how do these relate to immersive storytelling? Many of the storyworlds and storytelling projects we have recounted in this book rely in some way on digital platforms, indeed, often the very platforms that are being pinpointed within critiques about how we are observed, quantified, and made 'valuable' within the online space: Facebook, Twitter, YouTube, and Google for example. To participate in franchise storyworlds often means to give of one's data as one traverses the web of content across these (and other) platforms. Some theorists have gone as far as to question the kinds of labour being provided by fan communities and users of services/systems in the pursuit of content, experience, and immersion (Scholz 2012; Elder-vass 2016; Hassler-Forest 2016). Outside of any profit that might accrue to the producers of the storyworld's content there are other benefits of that labour that are accruing principally to the Silicon Valley companies whose platforms underpin that work. Users might happily and knowingly collude in such a system, seeing the benefits of participation as worthwhile, but many will be unaware of those connections.

Discussion at the intersections of technology and capitalism quickly turns then to talk about exploitation. Immersive storytelling – perhaps especially in the work of franchise storytelling and branding, and in mixed-media, multimedia, and interactive formats – navigates tricky territory where extensive and expansive ethical questions should be explored. This is especially pertinent at a time when data literacy and data justice (Dencik et al. 2016) are being catapulted onto the agenda by recent geopolitical developments.

Responding to the Charges

Some scholars have responded to these charges against immersion with agility and forcefulness. Lukas questions why these critiques assume that the outcomes of immersion will be 'inherently negative' (2016: 119), and asks why it is so difficult for critics to conceive of a willing, complicit, yet knowing, and critical participant in immersive encounters; 'not an agent acting upon or a subject being acted upon but an individual who is, along with all others, in the midst of things' (ibid: 119). Brian Lonsway introduces the notion of 'complicated agency' concluding that it is possible for a piece of work to be both 'empowering and disempowering, supportive and challenging of free will, educational and consumerist' (2016: 246). This notion of complicated agency is appealing given the criticisms above, and the variety of practice that we have referenced in this book. We have noted here that participation in immersive experience can often be connected to consumerism, neo-liberalism, and aesthetic capitalism. Yet, in interesting and quite profound ways, we have also seen it connected to practices that are more playful and political (and we

Against Immersion? 101

began to introduce some examples at the start of this chapter). To echo Matthew Causey's work from performance studies, more and more we may find artists and practitioners 'conversant with the language and conceptual frameworks' of the market, consumerism, and the digital, working within those languages and frameworks 'in order to respond, engage, and critique the systems of control' (2016: 431). In this view, immersive media might become themselves a part of the apparatus of resistance. This is indeed complicated agency.

In recognition of that, we would echo Dan Hassler-Forest's approach to the study of transmedia storyworlds that 'attempts to identify and acknowledge this radical potential without underestimating the powerful forces that contain it' (2016: 20–21). He goes on:

> Even as popular storyworlds are constantly being appropriated by capitalisms incontrovertible logic of accumulation, and as audiences' creative work is transformed into immaterial labor at the service of media corporations, there remains a valuable radical potential that is clearly worth salvaging.
>
> (2016: 4)

Examples of this radical potential include the World Economic Forum's VR experience ***Project Syria***, or ***The Letter***, which introduces participants to the life and experiences of Shaka Senghor who was incarcerated in Michigan for 19 years. Other examples include ***The Lost Palace***, a mixed-reality encounter on the streets of London that viscerally connects you with the past and ***Extinct*** which explores our right to a voice and to privacy. Here we see the affective dimensions of immersive media being utilised to different ends. The debate about neo-liberalism is not the whole story here then. Although on the one hand we have huge investment in slick VR outputs like the National History Museum's ***Hold The World*** project (with Sky VR Studio 2018) or AR offers like ***Pokémon Go***, there are also charities, arts, education, and community groups scratching together vibrant immersive projects on a shoestring.

But while this radical potential is certainly there, it is clear that strategies for creating immersive experiences can also be used for pure entertainment, escapism, and in the context of consumerism. Although some immersive experiences aim to challenge or educate (as some of the themed lands within Hong Kong's ***Ocean Park*** do with their ecological messaging), not all do. Many have mixed ambitions, and some are difficult to ascertain. In this complex field, it seems important that researchers remain open minded, non-judgemental, and work to draw up – and defend – their own distinctions. Off-hand dismissal of the remainder of the field as in some way inferior would seem shortsighted in the extreme, and ultimately unhelpful. Again, we make the case for criticality, whatever one's own research outputs, approach, or agenda.

Immersive storytelling is a mixed ecology and is supported by a mixed economy. It is complicated. As researchers we try and embrace and reflect that complexity in the way we write about our research, talk about it with participants, and produce our practice. Rather than eradicate that complexity or resolve it in some way, we advocate the approach proposed by Lukas when he suggests that 'it is incumbent on all of us—researchers, cultural critics, designers, operators, consultants, and guests—to appreciate and express the nuance, complexity, and ambiguity inherent in the idea of immersion' (Lukas 2016: 120). We are reminded again that it is through being attentive to the complex internalised processes of 'being' immersed that we gain access to the humanistic potentials of these forms. These are, for us, the most pertinent, radical, and challenging dynamics of immersive storytelling to be exploring at this time.

Summary

This chapter has explored the knottier extensions of debates about immersive storytelling. It has looked at four 'charges' against immersive practice: that its conceptualisation of agency is flawed; that it has been too far – and cynically – co-opted by mainstream culture; that it may lead to addictive behaviours; and that it is technocratic. It has then considered another way of thinking about these practices that embraces their complexity. It notes that these charges *might* be justifiable, but that they are not the whole story. We have introduced the concept of 'complicated agency' as a way of making sense of participation in immersive experiences, and proposed that there are examples of practice that demonstrate a radical potential for immersive storytelling, although not inevitably or indubitably.

In the following chapter, we offer some closing thoughts on the potency and importance of criticality in our engagements with immersive storytelling going forward.

Notes

1 This equivocacy underpins our decision to frame this discussion as a question rather than an assertion in the title of the chapter.
2 Currently articulated in the UK context as Advertising, Architecture, Arts and Culture, Craft, Creative Technologies, Design, Fashion, Games, Music, Publishing, TV, and Film (Creative Industries Council 2014).
3 Loton et al. suggest that further studies should be done to 'explore the role of coping in the relationships between other intense hobbies (including various media consumption) and mental health' (2016: unpaged).
4 Technodeterminism is, according to Bauchspies et al. 'the idea that technological change is inevitable and always "progress"' (2006: 10).
5 See also various chapters in the edited volume on *Digital Sociologies* (Daniels et al. 2017).

5 Conclusion

As we have seen in this book, doing 'something immersive' encompasses a complex field of occasions, media, participation, and creations. The aim of this book has been not only to encounter and introduce the many different modes and media of immersive storytelling that exist in our contemporary mediascape, but also to give readers some tools to approach research within what is evidently a fast changing environment, where nobody can be quite sure what the next big thing is going to be. This is the reason we decided to write a relatively short book but with a fast turnaround: these sectors change rapidly, and that is without even considering technological advances. We are confident that the discussions – and the framework – introduced within this book will be instructive, even as the particular projects, companies, and platforms we have used as examples here mutate over time, and perhaps even evolve into extinction.

We have outlined a systematic way of approaching immersive storytelling: defining it, describing it, analysing it, researching its impacts, and acknowledging its shortcomings. In short, we have introduced a mechanism for *critically* engaging with how stories are not just told but *made* through experiences. We have illustrated the discussions in this book with examples and presented a flexible approach that readers can adapt to utilise in their own research.

As outlined in Chapter 1, our approach has been expansive and not centred on digital technologies; we have been careful not to foreground the digital in the treatment of our subject here for reasons we have stated. There are simply too many exciting examples of immersive storytelling practice that are excluded by implementing such a limitation, and too much of the history is lost. In recognition of this complex field of both practice and study, we offered four different perspectives. We discussed the term 'immersion' as a liquid metaphor – and the consequences of its use in such a way.

Conclusion 105

We focused on 'experience' as an agent of immersion – reflecting on the balance of sensory experience and story in transporting participants into a different world. We explored the history of both the practices and the scholarship of deep immersion as a contemporary phenomenon; and lastly we drew our own definition that reflects this expansive approach, incorporating as it does both bounded encounters with story, and more extensive and layered storyworlds. We hope that our definition will prompt and provoke discussion, for others would no doubt have defined it differently.

None of the research approaches or frameworks that we had previously encountered did what we needed them to in terms of allowing us to flexibly yet systematically analyse the complex, multilayered phenomenon of an immersive storytelling experience, not to mention whole storyworlds. We therefore developed our own approach that can be applied flexibly within numerous different contexts. The Layers of Experience framework introduced in Chapter 2 used the *Harry Potter* storyworld as an illustration to explore the immersive qualities of different genres, and in so doing, demonstrated how the complex layering of experience can be prised open for analysis. We initially considered experiences as a very broad concept, to demonstrate how to tease out both the storytelling and immersive aspects some experiences have. Focusing on the different orientations of participant, process, and creation allowed us to consider how story (our fourth orientation) grew out of the intersections of the former three. We treated the immersive aspects of each orientation as an additional dimension, something that can be encoded in parts of an experience. This framework, through its layered approach, allows researchers to investigate the concept of deep immersion from both a physical (mostly found in layers dedicated to the exploration of the creation) and a conceptual perspective (mostly found in layers dedicated to the story).

In Chapter 3, we demonstrated how this approach could be used as a way of critically engaging with one case study: ***Traces***. This case study lent itself to an insightful exploration of the affective, spatial, sensorial, and embodied dimensions of immersion, as well as the processes that underpinned its creation. We showed different ways to approach researching an experience in order to judge whether it could be considered an example of immersive storytelling, ranging from participant interviews (with our feet firmly planted on the glass-bottomed boat, to return to our analogy in Chapter 1) to research carried out as participant (dipping into the ocean ourselves). Here we demonstrated the triangulation of different orientations to arrive at a point of reflection on *Traces* as immersive story.

In this book, we have also considered how immersive storytelling intersects with broader debates about society, economics, politics, and power. In Chapter 4, we noted different trajectories for practice within the field of immersive storytelling, ones that aligned more straightforwardly with consumerism and notions of 'experience', and others which opened up space for radicality and more searching social critique. Immersive stories can – and do – operate in all of those spaces simultaneously. They are dynamic and energetic. This is what makes them exciting terrain, and such a rich site for research. Referencing Brian Lonsway (2016), we introduced the concept of 'complicated agency' as one way of articulating the multiplicity and multidimensionality of immersive storytelling forms, and in particular the practices of participation that they facilitate.

With the decision to write a short book came the need to narrow our focus, and there are many avenues within immersive storytelling that have not been explored within these pages. Our treatment of the history of immersive storytelling has been sufficient for our needs, but there is appetite for more detailed scholarly work on this, and although not congruent given our approach in this book, there is definitely scope to explore particular kinds of practice in more detail. Immersive journalism, street gaming, escape rooms, and immersive heritage for example have not undergone detailed scholarly enquiry, unlike transmedia storytelling, immersive theatre, and Virtual Reality gaming which have received more attention.

This book makes the case for critical encounters with immersive storytelling practice. It does so against a backdrop of increased (uncritical) use of the term 'immersion' within a range of contexts, and a broader narrative turn within culture and across society. We have offered a way into that critique, a reasoning, a language, a framework, and real-world examples. We hope that this will be instructive to others who find themselves working, researching, or studying in this space. Readers should be minded always to ask how this term 'immersion' is being activated, and to what ends, and to explore what kinds of stories (including *whose* stories) are being privileged. Overall, we hope that this book has demonstrated that immersion is more – and more complex – than its liquid metaphor roots suggest. It is not just a matter of richly designed environments (whether virtual or analogue), but the important role that story plays in allowing participants to explore an idea, a concept, or a whole world that makes immersive storytelling experiences special.

Bibliography

Abbott, P. (2008) 'Genre bending and utopia-building', *Critical Review of Intermedial Social and Political Philosophy*, 11(3), pp. 335–346.

Adams, E. (2014) *Fundamentals of Games Design*. 3rd edn. Berkeley, CA: New Riders.

Alcorn, S. (2014) 'Tips for writing your script', *Tejix Technology for Theme Parks*, 23 August 2014. Available at: https://web.archive.org/web/20140823193203/, www.tejix.com/en/PaperPlot.html (Accessed: 25 July 2018).

Alston, A. (2013) 'Audience participation and neoliberal value: risk, agency and responsibility in immersive theatre', *Performance Research*, 18(2), pp. 128–138.

Ambient Literature. (2016) 'About the project'. Available at: https://ambientlit.com/index.php/about-the-project/ (Accessed: 5 September 2018).

Ang, I. (1995) *Living Room Wars: Rethinking Media Audiences for a Post-Modern World*. New York: Routledge.

Barthes, R. (1977) *Image, Music, Text: Essays Selected and Translated [from the French] by Stephen Heath*. London: Fontana Press.

Bauchspies, W.K., Croissant, J. and Restivo, S. (2006) *Science, Technology and Society*. Malden, MA, Oxford and Victoria: Blackwell Publishing.

Bean, A.M., Nielsen, R.K.L., van Rooij, A.J. and Ferguson, C.J. (2017) 'Video game addiction: the push to pathologize video games', *Professional Psychology: Research and Practice*, 48(5), pp. 378–389.

Benjamin, W. (1955) *Illuminations*. Edited and with an introduction by Hannah Arendt; translated by Harry Zohn. London: Fontana.

Bennett, S. (1990) *Theatre Audiences*. London: Routledge.

Bertin, J. (2001) 'Matrix theory of graphics', *Information Design Journal*, 10(1), pp. 5–19.

Birkerts, S. (1994) *The Gutenberg Elegies: The Fate of Reading in an Electronic Age*. Boston, MA: Faber and Faber.

Bishop, C. (2012) *Artificial Hells: Participatory Art and the Politics of Spectatorship*. London and New York: Verso.

Bobo, J. (1995) *The Colour Purple: Black Women as Cultural Readers*. New York and Chichester: Columbia University Press.

Böhme, G. (2017) *Critique of Aesthetic Capitalism*. Translated by Edmund Jephcott. (sine loco): Mimesis International.

Booker, C. (2005) *The Seven Basic Plots: Why We Tell Stories*. London and New York: Continuum.

Boucher, G. (2011) '"Harry Potter": Did 3-D really make the film more magical?', *Hero Complex*. 29 July. Available at: http://herocomplex.latimes.com/movies/harry-potter-did-3d-really-make-the-film-more-magical/ (Accessed: 28 April 2018).

Bourdieu, P. (1997) 'The forms of capital', in Halsey, A.H., Lauder, H. and Brown, P. (eds.) *Education: Culture, Economy, Society*. Oxford: Oxford University Press, pp. 46–58.

British Library (ed.) (2017) *Harry Potter: A History of Magic* [exhibition catalogue]. London, Oxford, New York, New Delhi, and Sydney: Bloomsbury Publishing.

Brownie, B. (2006) 'A brief introduction to Gestalt, identifying key theories and principles', *FluidType*. Available at: http://fluidtype.org/texts/Gestalt%20Theories%20and%20Principles.pdf (Accessed: 8 February 2018).

Bucher, J. (2017) *Storytelling for Virtual Reality: Methods and Principles*. New York and Oxon: Routledge.

Burgess, J. and Green, J. (2018) *YouTube: Online Video and Participatory Culture*. Cambridge: Polity Press.

Campbell, J. (2012) *The Hero with a Thousand Faces*. 3rd edn. Novato, CA: New World Library.

Candy, L. (2014) 'Evaluation and experience in art', in Candy, L. and Ferguson, S. (eds.) *Interactive Experience in the Digital Age: Evaluating New Art Practice*. London: Springer, pp. 25–48.

Candy, L. and Ferguson, S. (eds.) (2014) *Interactive Experience in the Digital Age: Evaluating New Art Practice*. London: Springer.

Carpentier, N. (2011) *Media and Participation: A Site of Ideological-Democratic Struggle*. Bristol: Intellect.

Carson, E. (2015) 'Immersive journalism: what virtual reality means for the future of storytelling and empathy-casting', *TechRepublic*. Available at: www.techrepublic.com/article/immersive-journalism-what-virtual-reality-means-for-the-future-of-storytelling-and-empathy-casting/ (Accessed: 17 July 2018).

Causey, M. (2016) 'Postdigital performance', *Theatre Journal*, 68(3), pp. 427–441.

Chitwood, A. (2016) '"Fantastic beasts' director David Yates explains what makes J.K. Rowling a unique screenwriter', *Collider*. 12 September. Available at: http://collider.com/fantastic-beasts-and-where-to-find-them-jk-rowling-screenwriter/ (Accessed: 22 July 2018).

Ciolfi, L. (2017) 'Physical-digital technologies for culture and heritage', *digital leaders*. 23 October. Available at: http://digileaders.com/physical-digital-technologies-culture-heritage/ (Accessed: 28 April 2018).

Ciolfi, L. and McLoughlin, M. (2017) 'Supporting place-specific interaction through a physical/digital assembly', *Human-Computer Interaction*, 33(5–6), pp. 499–543.

Cooke, B. and Kothari, U. (2001) *Participation: The New Tyranny?* London and New York: Zed Books.
Cooper, E. and Dinerman, H. (1951) 'Analysis of the film *Don't be a Sucker*: a study in communication', *Public Opinion Quarterly*, 15, pp. 243–264.
Creative Industries Council. (2014) 'Industries'. Available at: www.thecreativeindustries.co.uk/industries (Accessed: 4 September 2018).
Csikszentmihalyi, M. (1990) *Flow: The Psychology of Optimal Experience*. New York: Harper and Row.
Daniels, J., Gregory, K. and McMillan Cottom, T. (2017) *Digital Sociologies*. Bristol and Chicago, IL: Policy Press.
Debord, G. (1967) *La société du spectacle*. Paris: Buchet-Chastel.
Deleuze, J., Long, J., Liu, T., Maurage, P. and Billieux, J. (2018) 'Passion or addiction? Correlates of healthy versus problematic use of videogames in a sample of French-speaking regular players', *Addictive Behaviors*, 82, pp. 114–121.
Dencik, L. and Cable, J. (2017) 'The advent of surveillance realism: public opinion and activist responses to the Snowden leaks', *International Journal of Communication*, 11, pp. 763–781.
Dencik, L., Hintz, A. and Cable, J. (2016) 'Towards data justice? The ambiguity of anti-surveillance resistance in political activism', *Big Data and Society*, 3(2), pp. 1–12.
Derrida, J. (1980) 'The law of genre', translated by Avital Ronell, *Critical Inquiry*, 7(1), pp. 55–81.
Dinesh, N. (2016) *Memos from a Theatre Lab: Exploring What Immersive Theatre 'Does'*. New York and Oxon: Routledge.
Duffett, M. (2013) *Understanding Fandom: An Introduction to the Study of Media Fan Culture*. New York and London: Bloomsbury.
Elder-Vass, D. (2016) *Profit and Gift in the Digital Economy*. Cambridge: Cambridge University Press.
Elliott, K. (2014) 'Doing adaptation: the adaptation as critic', in Cartmell, D. and Whelehan, I. (eds.) *Teaching Adaptations*. Basingstoke: Palgrave MacMillan, pp. 71–86.
English, F. (2012) *Student Writing and Genre: Reconfiguring Academic Knowledge*. London: Bloomsbury [first published in 2011 by Continuum].
Farman, J. (2015) 'Stories, spaces, and bodies: the production of embodied space through mobile media storytelling', *Communication Research and Practice*, 1(2), pp. 101–116.
Farman, J. (ed.) (2014b) *The Mobile Story: Narrative Practices with Locative Technologies*. New York and London: Routledge.
Farman, J. (2014a) 'Storytelling with mobile media: exploring the intersection of site-specificity, content, and materiality', in Goggin, G. and Hjort, L. (eds.) *The Routledge Companion to Mobile Media*. New York and Oxon: Routledge, pp. 528–537.
Finnegan, R. (1997) 'Storying the self: personal narratives and identity', in McKay, H. (ed.) *Consumption and Everyday Life*. London: Sage, pp. 65–112.
Fish, A. (2017) *Technoliberalism and the End of Participatory Culture in the United States*. Cham: Palgrave Macmillan.

Foucault, M. (1981) *The History of Sexuality*. New York and Toronto: Vintage Books, Random House.
Foucault, M. (1979) *Discipline and Punish: The Birth of the Prison*. New York and Toronto: Vintage Books, Random House.
Freshwater, H. (2009) *Theatre and Audience*. Hampshire and New York: Palgrave Macmillan.
Freytag, G. (1896) *Freytag's Techniques of Drama: An Exposition of Dramatic Composition and Art*. Reprint of 2nd edition. London: Forgotten Books, 2012.
Frost, J. (2017) 'Is addiction to Disney theme parks and actual thing? If so, I have it', *The Disney Blog*. 10 July. Available at: https://thedisneyblog.com/2017/07/10/addiction-disney-theme-parks-actual-thing/ (Accessed: 10 August 2018).
Galani, A. and Kidd, J. (forthcoming, 2019) 'Evaluating digital cultural heritage 'in the wild': the case for reflexivity', *Journal on Computing and Cultural Heritage*.
Galindo, A.S. (2014) 'Mobile media after 9/11: the September 11 memorial and museum app', in Farman, J. (ed.) *The Mobile Story: Narrative Practices with Locative Technologies*. New York and London: Routledge, pp. 263–275.
Gardner, H.E. (1995) *Leading Minds: An Anatomy of Leadership*. New York: Basic Books.
Gillespie, M. (1995) *Television, Ethnicity and Cultural Change*. London and New York: Routledge.
Goffman, E. (1956) *The Presentation of Self in Everyday Life*. Edinburgh: University of Edinburgh Social Sciences Research Centre.
Greenfield, P. (2018) 'The Cambridge Analytica files: the story so far', *The Guardian*. 26 March. Available at: www.theguardian.com/news/2018/mar/26/the-cambridge-analytica-files-the-story-so-far (Accessed: 10 May 2018).
Griffiths, A. (2008) *Shivers Down Your Spine: Cinema, Museums, and the Immersive View*. New York and Chichester: Columbia University Press.
Gröppel-Wegener, A. (2018) 'Embodying regenring: analysing the Genre Furoshiki using English's theoretical framework', *Journal of Writing in Creative Practice*, 11(1), pp. 13–37.
Gröppel-Wegener, A. (2011) 'Creating heritage experiences through architecture', in Jackson, A. and Kidd, J. (eds.) *Performing Heritage: Research, Practice and Innovation in Museum Theatre and Live Interpretation*. Manchester and New York: Manchester University Press, pp. 39–52.
Harrison, J. (2017) 'Introduction', in British Library (ed.) *Harry Potter: A History of Magic* [exhibition catalogue]. London, Oxford, New York, New Delhi, and Sydney: Bloomsbury Publishing, pp. 8–14.
Harvey, C., Ryan, M. and Thon, J. (2014) *Storyworlds across Media: Toward a Media-Conscious Narratology*. Lincoln and London: University of Nebraska Press.

Bibliography 111

Hassler-Forest, D. (2016) *Science Fiction, Fantasy, and Politics: Transmedia World-Building beyond Capitalism*. London and New York: Rowman and Littlefield.
Hayles, N. K., Jagoda, P. and LeMieux, P. (2014) 'Speculation: financial games and derivative worlding in a transmedia era', *Critical Inquiry*, 40(3), pp. 220–236.
Hellekson, K. and Busse, K. (2014) *The Fan Fiction Studies Reader*. Iowa City: University of Iowa Press.
Herman, D. (2002) *Story Logic: Problems and Possibilities of Narrative*. Lincoln and London: University of Nebraska Press.
Hills, M. (2002) *Fan Cultures*. Oxon: Routledge.
Horkheimer, M. and Adorno, T.W. (1955) *The Dialectic of Enlightenment*. 2000 edition. Stanford, CA: Stanford University Press.
Hutter, M. (2016) 'Book review of *Aesthetic Capitalism*', *Thesis Eleven*, 132(1), pp. 128–132.
Huws, S., John, A. and Kidd, J. (forthcoming, 2019) '*Traces – Olion*: creating a bilingual 'subtlemob' for National Museum Wales', in Lewi, H., Smith, W. and Cooke, S. (eds.) *The Routledge International Handbook of New Digital Practices in Galleries, Libraries, Archives, Museums and Heritage Sites*. New York and London: Routledge.
Jackson, A. (2011) 'Engaging the audience: negotiating performance in the Museum', in Jackson, A. and Kidd, J. (eds.) *Performing Heritage: Research, Practice and Innovation in Museum Theatre and Live Interpretation*. Manchester and New York: Manchester University Press, pp. 11–25.
Jenkins, H. (1992) *Textual Poachers: Television Fans and Participatory Culture*. London and New York: Routledge.
Jenkins, H., Ford, S. and Green, J. (2013) *Spreadable Media: Creating Value and Meaning in a Networked Culture*. New York: New York University Press.
Jhally, S. and Lewis, J. (1992) *Enlightened Racism: The Cosby Show, Audiences, and the Myth of the American Dream*. Boulder, CO: Westview Press.
Katz, E. and Liebes, T. (1993) *The Export of Meaning: Cross-Cultural Readings of Dallas*. 2nd edn. Cambridge, UK and Cambridge, MA: Polity Press.
Keil, J., Pujol, L., Roussou, M., Engelke, T., Schmitt, M., Bockholt, U. and Eleftheratou, S. (2013) 'A digital look at physical museum exhibits: designing personalized stories with handheld augmented reality in museums', in *Proceedings of the Digital Heritage International Congress, Volume 2*. Piscataway, NJ: IEEE, pp. 685–688.
Kenderdine, S. (2016) 'Embodiment, entanglement, and immersion in digital cultural heritage', in Schreibman, S., Siemens, R. and Unsworth, J. (eds.) *A New Companion to Digital Humanities*. Chichester and Malden, MA: John Wiley and Sons Ltd, pp. 22–41.
Kidd, J. (2018b) 'Transmedia heritage', in Freeman, M. and Gambarato, R.R. (eds.) *The Routledge Companion to Transmedia Studies*. New York and Oxon: Routledge, pp. 272–278.

Kidd, J. (2018a) '"Immersive' heritage encounters', *The Museum Review* 3(1), pp. 1–16.
Kidd, J. (2017) '*With New Eyes I See*: embodiment, empathy and silence in digital heritage interpretation', *International Journal of Heritage Studies*. Available at: www.tandfonline.com/doi/pdf/10.1080/13527258.2017.1341946?needAccess=true (Accessed: 31 August 2018).
Kidd, J. (2011) 'The costume of openness: heritage performance as a participatory cultural practice', in Jackson, A. and Kidd, J. (eds.) *Performing Heritage*. Manchester: Manchester University Press, pp. 204–219.
Kitchin, R., Lauriault, T.P. and Wilson, M.W. (2017) *Understanding Spatial Media*. London, Thousand Oaks, CA, New Delhi, and Singapore: SAGE.
Kleinhenz, M.N. (no date) 'Harry Potter: Gringotts Original Ride Story was Scrapped', *Orlando Informer*. Available at: https://orlandoinformer.com/blog/gringotts-original-story-scrapped/ (Accessed: 23 July 2018).
Kluft, D. (2015) 'Harry Potter Lawsuits and Where to Find them', *Trademark and Copyright Law blog*. 27 July. Available at: www.trademarkandcopyrightlawblog.com/2015/07/harry-potter-lawsuits-and-where-to-find-them/ (Accessed: 23 July 2018).
Kuzmičová, A. Schilhab, T. and Burke, M. (2018) 'm-Reading: fiction reading from mobile phones', *Convergence: The International Journal of Research into New Media Technology*. Available at: http://journals.sagepub.com/doi/pdf/10.1177/1354856518770987 (Accessed: 31 August 2018).
Lash, S. (2006) 'Experience', *Theory, Culture and Society*, 23(2–3), pp. 335–341.
Livingstone, S. (2013) 'The participation paradigm in audience research', *The Communication Review*, 16, pp. 21–30.
Lonsway, B. (2016) 'Complicated agency', in Lukas, S.A. (ed.) *A Reader in Themed and Immersive Spaces*. (sine loco): ETC Press, pp. 239–248.
Lorek-Jezinska, E. (2002) 'Audience activating techniques and their educational efficacy', *Applied Theatre Researcher*, 3, Article 6 (unpaged).
Loton, D., Borkoles, E., Lubman, D. and Polman, R.C.J. (2016) 'Video game addiction, engagement and symptoms of stress, depression and anxiety: the mediating role of coping', *International Journal of Mental Health and Addiction*, 14(4), pp. 565–578. Submitted author's copy available at: https://eprints.qut.edu.au/105905/ (Accessed: 10 August 2018).
Lukas, S.A. (2016) 'Introduction: the meanings of themed and immersive spaces', in Lukas, S.A. (ed.) *A Reader in Themed and Immersive Spaces* (sine loco): ETC Press. pp. 3–15.
Lukas, S.A. (2013) *The Immersive Worlds Handbook: Designing Theme Parks and Consumer Spaces*. New York and London: Focal Press.
Machon, J. (2013) *Immersive Theatres: Intimacy and Immediacy in Contemporary Performance*. Hampshire and New York: Palgrave Macmillan.
Machon, J. (2009) *(Syn)aesthetics: Redefining Visceral Performance*. Hampshire and New York: Palgrave Macmillan.
Mandal, A. (2015) 'Gothic 2.0: remixing revenants in the transmedia age', in Piatti-Farnell, L. and Brien, D.L. (eds.) *New Directions in 21st-Century Gothic: The Gothic Compass. Routledge Interdisciplinary Perspectives on Literature*. London and New York: Routledge, pp. 84–100.

Mangen, A. (2008) 'Hypertext fiction reading: haptics and immersion', *Journal of Research in Reading*, 31(4), pp. 404–419.
Mangen, A. and van der Weel, A. (2017) 'Why don't we read hypertext novels?', *Convergence*, 23(2), pp. 166–181.
Marling, K.A. (1997) 'Imagineering the Disney theme park', in Marling, K.A. (ed.) *Designing Disney's Theme Parks – The Architecture of Reassurance*. Paris and New York: Flammarion, pp. 29–178.
Marx, K. (1867) *Capital: Vol. 1: The Process of Production of Capital*. Moscow: Progress Publishers.
McAdams, D.P. (1993) *The Stories We Live By: Personal Myths and the Making of the Self*. New York and London: The Guildford Press.
McErlean, K. (2018) *Interactive Narratives and Transmedia Storytelling: Creating Immersive Stories Across New Media Platforms*. New York and London: Routledge.
McLuhan, M. (1964) *Understanding Media: The Extensions of Man*. 2001 edition. London: Routledge.
McMahon, A. (2003) 'Immersion, engagement, and presence: a method for analyzing 3-D video games', in Wolf, M.J.P. and Perron, B. (eds.) *The Video Game Theory Reader*. New York: Routledge, Taylor & Francis Group, pp. 77–78.
McStay, A. (2016) *Digital Advertising*. 2nd edn. London: Palgrave Macmillan.
Moloney, K. (2012) Postdigital narrative. 'Transmedia Journalism as a Post-Digital Narrative'. Available at: www.colorado.edu/journalism/photojournalism/Transmedia_Journalism_as_a_Post-Digtal_Narrative.pdf (Accessed: 5 September 2018).
Morley, D. (1980) *The Nationwide Audience: Structure and Decoding*. London: British Film Institute.
Morozov, E. (2011) *The Net Delusion: How Not to Liberate the World*. London: Allen Lane.
Mosse, D. (2001) ''People's knowledge', participation and patronage: operations and representations in rural development', in Cooke, B. and Kothari, U. (eds.) *Participation: The New Tyranny?* London and New York: Zed Books, pp. 16–35.
Murphy, P. (2014) 'The aesthetic spirit of modern capitalism', in Murphy, P. and de la Fuente, E. (eds.) *Aesthetic Capitalism*. Leiden: Brill, pp. 47–62.
Murphy, P. and de la Fuente, E. (2014) *Aesthetic Capitalism*. Leiden: Brill.
Murray, J. (1997) *Hamlet on the Holodeck: The Future of Narrative in Cyberspace*. Cambridge, MA: The MIT Press.
National Museum Wales (2016) 'Traces app', *museum.wales*. Available at: https://museum.wales/stfagans/whatson/traces/ (Accessed: 14 August 2018).
Nocera, J. (2008) 'Who owns how much of Harry Potter?', *New York Times Online*. 9 February. Available at: www.nytimes.com/2008/02/09/business/worldbusiness/09iht-wbjoe09.4.9893157.html (Accessed: 23 July 2018).
Oh, L.H. (2018) 'The 8 genius hacks you need to know before visiting Harry Potter world', *Real Simple*. 12 April. Available at:

www.realsimple.com/work-life/travel/harry-potter-world (Accessed: 25 July 2018).
Ohta, Y. and Tamura, H. (1999) *Mixed Reality: Merging Real and Virtual Worlds*. Berlin and Heidelberg: Springer Verlag.
Ong, W.J. (1982) *Orality and Literacy: The Technology of the Word*. 2002 edn. London: Routledge.
Page, R.E. (2018) *Narratives Online: Shared Stories in Social Media*. Cambridge: Cambridge University Press.
Page, R.E. (2012) *Stories and Social Media: Identities and Interaction*. New York and Oxon: Routledge.
Palace Theatre London (ed.) (2018) *Harry Potter and the Cursed Child* [programme booklet, February 2018]. London: Dewynters.
Paterson, R. (2002) 'Television: a framework for analysing contemporary television', in Briggs, A. and Cobley, P. (eds.) *The Media: An Introduction*. 2nd edn. Essex: Pearson Education Ltd, pp. 135–147.
Petrelli, D., Ciolfi, L., van Dijk, D., Hornecker, E., Not, E. and Schmidt, A. (2013) 'Integrating material and digital: a new way for cultural heritage', *Interactions*, 20(4), pp. 58–63.
Pine, B.J. and Gilmore, J.H. (1998) 'Welcome to the experience economy', *Harvard Business Review*, July–August 1998, unpaged. Available at: https://hbr.org/1998/07/welcome-to-the-experience-economy (Accessed: 9 August 2018).
Poole, S. (2017) 'Ghosts in the garden: locative gameplay and historical interpretation from below', *International Journal of Heritage Studies*, 24(3), pp. 300–314.
Pottermore News Team (2018) 'Natalie Dormer to join the Wizarding World with History of Magic audiobook', *Pottermore*. 9 August. Available at: www.pottermore.com/news/natalie-dormer-to-join-the-wizarding-world-with-history-of-magic-audiobook (Accessed: 9 August 2018).
Propp, V. (1971) *Morphology of the Folk Tale*. 2nd rev. edn. Austin: University of Texas Press.
Pullinger, K. (2018) 'Breathe', *KatePullinger*. Available at: www.katepullinger.com/breathe/ (Accessed: 22 August 2018).
Qu, K. (2017) 'The impact of experience on satisfaction and revisit intention in theme parks: an application of the experience economy', *Graduate Theses and Dissertations*. 15609. Available at: https://lib.dr.iastate.edu/etd/15609 (Accessed: 9 August 2018).
Rancière, J. (2009) *The Emancipated Spectator*. London and New York: Verso.
Ratcliffe, R. (2016) 'JK Rowling tells of anger at attacks on casting of black Hermione', *The Observer*. 5 June. Available at: www.theguardian.com/stage/2016/jun/05/harry-potter-jk--rowling-black-hermione (Accessed: 25 July 2018).
Reason, M. (2015) 'Participations on participation: researching the 'active' theatre audience', *Participations*, 12(1), pp. 271–280.
Redden, J. and Brand, J. (2017) 'Data harm record', *Data Justice Lab*. Available at: https://datajustice.files.wordpress.com/2017/12/data-harm-record-djl2.pdf (Accessed: 10 May 2018).

Reed, T.V. (2014) *Digitized Lives: Culture, Power and Social Change in the Internet Era*. New York and London: Routledge.

Rieser, M. (ed.) (2011) *The Mobile Audience: Media Art and Mobile Technologies*. Amsterdam and New York: Rodopi.

Rieser, M. (2005) 'Locative media and spatial narrative', *REFRESH conference*, Banff Center, Sept 29–Oct 4. Available at: http://locative.articule.net/wp-content/uploads/2013/06/Reiser_LocativeMediaSpatialNarrative.pdf (Accessed: 30 April 2018).

Ritchie, J. (2014) 'The affordances and constraints of mobile locative narratives', in Farman, J. (ed.) *The Mobile Story: Narrative Practices with Locative Technologies*. New York and London: Routledge, pp. 53–67.

Rose, F. (2011) *The Art of Immersion: How the Digital Generation Is Remaking Hollywood, Madison Avenue, and the Way We Tell Stories*. New York and London: W.W. Norton and Company, Inc.

Rowling, J.K., Tiffany, J. and Thorne, J. (2016) *Harry Potter and the Cursed Child – Parts One and Two: The Official Script Book of the Original West End Production (Special Rehearsal Edition)* New York: Arthur A Levine Books.

Ryan, M. (2004) *Narrative across Media: The Language of Storytelling*. Lincoln and London: University of Nebraska Press.

Ryan, M., Foote, K. and Azaryahu, M. (2016) *Narrating Space/Spatializing Narrative: Where Narrative and Geography Meet*. Columbus: The Ohio State University.

Ryan, M. and Thon, J. (2014) (eds.) *Storyworlds across Media: Toward a Media-Conscious Narratology*. Lincoln and London: University of Nebraska Press.

Schechner, R. (1973) *Environmental Theatre*. New York: Applause Books.

Schmitt, B. (1999) 'Experiential marketing', *Journal of Marketing Management*, 15(1–3), pp. 53–67.

Scholz, T. (2012) *Digital Labor*. New York and London: Routledge.

Seah, M. and Cairns, P. (2008) 'From immersion to addiction in videogames', *People and Computers XXII, Culture, Creativity, Interaction*; Proceedings from HCI 2008, Liverpool John Moores University, 1–5 September 2008, Liverpool John Moores University. Available at: https://ewic.bcs.org/content/ConWebDoc/21343 (Accessed: 9 August 2018).

Secret Cinema (no date) 'About', *Secret Cinema*. Available at: www.secretcinema.org/about/ (Accessed: 21 August 2018).

Shaughnessy, N. (2012) *Applying Performance: Live Art, Socially Engaged Theatre and Affective Practice*. Hampshire and New York: Palgrave Macmillan.

Slater, M. and Wilbur, S. (1997) 'A framework for immersive virtual environments (FIVE): speculations on the role of presence in virtual environments', *Presence: Teleoperators and Virtual Environments*, 6(6), pp. 603–616.

Sloane, S. (2000) *Digital Fictions: Storytelling in a Material World*. Stamford, CT: Ablex Publishers.

Spencer, D. (2017) 'Work in and beyond the second machine age: the politics of production and digital technologies', *Work, Employment and Society*, 3(1), pp. 142–152.

Srnicek, N. (2017) *Platform Capitalism*. Cambridge, MA: Polity Press.
Stam, R. (2005) 'Introduction: the theory and practice of adaptation', in Stam, R. and Raengo, A. (eds.) *Literature and Film: A Guide to the Theory and Practice of Film Adaptation*. Malden, MA: Blackwell, pp. 1–52.
Steinicke, F. (2016) *Being Really Virtual: Immersive Natives and the Future of Virtual Reality*. Switzerland: Springer International Publishing.
Sundararajan, A. (2017) *The Sharing Economy: The End of Employment and the Rise of Crowd-Based Capitalism*. Cambridge, MA and London: MIT Press.
Therrien, A. (2018) 'WHO gaming disorder listing a 'moral panic', say experts', *BBC News*. Available at: www.bbc.com/news/health-44560338 (Accessed: 22 August 2018).
Toolan, M.J. (1988) *Narrative: A Critical Linguistic Introduction*. London: Routledge.
Triberti, S., Milani, L., Villani, D., Grumi, S., Peracchia, S., Curcio, G. and Riva, G. (2018) 'What matters is when you play: investigating the relationship between online video games addiction and time spent playing over specific day phases', *Addictive Behaviors Reports*. Corrected proof available at: www.sciencedirect.com/science/article/pii/S235285321830035X (Accessed: 30 August 2018).
Turner, F. (2018) 'The arts at Facebook: an aesthetic infrastructure for surveillance capitalism', *Poetics*, 67, pp. 53–62.
Warren, J. (2017) *Creating Worlds: How to make Immersive Theatre*. London: Nick Hern Books.
White, G. (2012) 'On immersive theatre', *Theatre Research International*, 37(3), pp. 221–235.
Wilkie, F. (2002) 'Mapping the terrain: a survey of site-specific performance in Britain', *New Theatre Quarterly*, 18(2), pp. 140–160.
Wolf, M.J.P. (2012) *Building Imaginary Worlds: The Theory and History of Subcreation*. New York and London: Routledge.
World Health Organization (2018) '6C51 gaming disorder', *ICD-11 for Mortality and Morbidity Statistics*. Available at: https://icd.who.int/browse11/l-m/en#/http://id.who.int/icd/entity/1448597234 (Accessed: 17 August 2018).
Yilmaz, R. and Ciğerci, F.M. (2018) 'A brief history of storytelling: from primitive dance to digital narration', in Yilmaz, R., Erdem, M.N. and Resuloğlu, F. (eds.) *Handbook of Research on Transmedia Storytelling and Narrative Strategies*. Hershey, PA: Information Science Reference Group, pp. 1–14.
Younger, D. (2016) *Theme Park Design & the Art of Themed Entertainment*. (sine loco): Inklingwood Press.
Zuboff, S. (2017) *The Age of Surveillance Capitalism: The Fight for a Human Future at the New Frontier of Power*. New York: PublicAffairs.

Glossary of Examples

This glossary offers brief overviews of examples used within the book. They correspond to those highlighted in bold throughout, and we offer web URLs where possible so that further information about them can be found.

The examples used in Chapter 2, which specifically relate to the *Harry Potter* discussion, are located in a dedicated section at the end of this Glossary.

Augmented Immersive Team Trainer, **US Marines 2016**

As a supplement to traditional training methods, there are now a number of examples of immersive media use within military contexts. The *Augmented Immersive Team Trainer* was one such prototype. The logic underpinning this work is that VR and AR scenarios can help train soldiers for real-world combat situations and teach them how to respond in a manner appropriate to the scenario. It can introduce soldiers to challenging and hostile climates and experiences without any of the risks involved. These programmes of course raise interesting questions about the relationship between experience and cognition, ethics, and the uses of military technology.

Bordergame, **National Theatre Wales and The Space 2014**

Bordergame was an immersive theatre experience that explored national borders, citizenship, and the status and experience of refugees. It had both an online and offline dimension, and sought to work across both. Participants journeyed by train from Bristol to Newport as refugees (across the England–Wales border) and had to convince border guards to let them in. Online participants – a volunteer army of Active Citizens – monitored the borders and decided the fate

118 *Glossary of Examples*

of those on the trains. *Bordergame* won the inaugural Space Prize Digital Theatre Award. More information at www.nationaltheatre wales.org/ntw_shows/bordergame/ (Accessed: 18 August 2018).

Breathe, Kate Pullinger, Ambient Literature, Visual Editions, and Google Creative Lab Sydney 2018

Breathe is a 'literary experience' accessed via smartphone (on mobile web rather than an app). It is a personalised experience that uses data from the world around readers to inform its ghostly narrative: location, time of day, and weather for example. More information at www.katepullinger.com/breathe/ (Accessed: 22 August 2018).

Extinct, Produced by yello brick with Wales Millennium Centre 2018

Extinct was conceived as a 'mixture of game and theatrical happenings' that played out on the streets of Cardiff in 2018. It moved between digital and analogue experiences, hybridising the two into an exploration of the place of technology within our everyday lives and our uses of data. More information at https://festivalofvoice.wales/whatson/extinct (Accessed: 11 May 2018).

Hold the World, Natural History Museum, UK and Sky VR Studio 2018

Hold the World is a VR experience using head-mounted display that takes you 'behind the scenes' of the Natural History Museum, into the collection spaces that are normally out of bounds for the visiting public, and offers them a chance to 'handle' the objects. The experience is hosted by well-known natural history broadcaster Sir David Attenborough who is digitally recreated for the experience as a 3D hologram. More information at www.nhm.ac.uk/discover/news/2018/march/explore-the-museum-with-sir-david-attenborough.html (Accessed: 11 May 2018).

Hunger in Los Angeles, Nonny de la Peña 2012

Hunger in Los Angeles is a virtual reality journalistic film that uses real audio recordings to recreate an account of an emergency at a Los Angeles food bank where a man went into diabetic shock. As a participant you are implicated; through first-person perspective, you become one of those who waits with him in line. It is expressly political in its subject matter, and activist in its intentions; raising awareness and visibility for those who are disenfranchised within the local community. More information at http://emblematicgroup.com/experiences/hunger-in-la/ (Accessed: 22 August 2018).

i-Docs

The i-Docs project has, since 2011, been acting as a forum for debate and the sharing of practice in the field of interactive documentary. The project has held a number of symposia, including in March 2018 where there were a number of sessions on immersive documentary. Videos of presentations from events as well as other resources can be found on the project website. More information at http://i-docs.org/ (Accessed: 3 September 2018).

I Am A Man, Derek A. Ham 2017

I Am A Man is a VR storytelling experience that centres the experiences of those who fought for equality as part of the African-American Civil Rights Movement. Using first-person perspective, *I Am A Man* encourages participants to walk in the shoes of those who fought for freedom, and to interact with the environment. Its ambition is to offer people a compelling way into that history and to personalise it in a way that makes it more meaningful. It has since been installed at the National Civil Rights Museum. More information at www.iamamanvr.com/ (Accessed: 22 August 2018).

It's No Game, Oscar Sharp and Ross Goodwin 2017

It's No Game is a science fiction story written as part of the 48 Hour Film Challenge at the Sci-Fi London Film Festival. It stars actor David Hasselhoff as the Hoffbot, delivering lines that have been written by an algorithm. More information at https://arstechnica.com/gaming/2017/04/an-ai-wrote-all-of-david-hasselhoffs-lines-in-this-demented-short-film/ (Accessed: 22 August 2018).

Jekyll 2.0, Anthony Mandal (Cardiff University) and SlingShot 2013

Jekyll 2.0 was a pervasive media adaptation of Robert Louis Stevenson's *Strange Case of Dr. Jekyll and Mr Hyde* that used participants' biodata to shape their experience. More information at http://

old.react-hub.org.uk/books-and-print-sandbox/projects/2013/jekyll-20/ (Accessed: 18 June 2018), or in Mandal 2015.

The Letter, Jamie Wong (Project Empathy) 2016

The Letter introduces participants to the life and experiences of Shaka Senghor who was incarcerated in Michigan for 19 years. The VR experience enables participants to 'retrace his footsteps'. *The Letter* was honoured as 'Best in VR' at Digital Hollywood 2016. More information at www.projectempathyvr.com/the-letter/ (Accessed: 11 May 2018).

The Lost Palace, Historic Royal Palaces with Chomko & Rosier and Uninvited Guests 2016

The Lost Palace was an ambitious immersive heritage encounter that 're-created' the Palace of Whitehall, London, which burned to the ground in 1698. The experience made significant use of binaural (3D) sound as well as NFC tags and haptic technologies, most notably in a section of the narrative where the handheld device/torch became the eerily realistic beating heart of King Charles I, which participants were asked to carry back towards Banqueting House. More information at www.youtube.com/watch?v=QzfC_se0wPU (Accessed: 11 May 2018) and in Kidd (2018a).

The Masque of the Red Death, Punchdrunk and Battersea Arts Centre 2007–2008

The Masque of the Red Death was grounded in the works of Edgar Allan Poe and featured a cast of macabre characters and sequences. Participants in this immersive theatre experience wore masks, and were able to roam at will through the Battersea Arts Centre, which had been completely transformed. More information at www.punchdrunk.org.uk/masque-of-the-red-death/ (Accessed: 18 June 2018).

Museum View, Google Cultural Institute

Museum View offers users a means to explore museums and heritage sites from wherever in the world they happen to be. As such, according to the blurb, it 'transcends physical boundaries' by offering a 360 sense of (some of) the partner museums' spaces and collections. Partners in the project include the Museo Frida Kahlo in Mexico, the Rijksmuseum, Netherlands, the National Museum – New Delhi, and Vancouver Art Gallery. More information at www.google.com/culturalinstitute/about/users/ (Accessed: 18 June 2018).

Ocean Park, Hong Kong

A theme park located on Hong Kong Island, which consists of eight different themed lands. Its mission is in its motto: 'connect people with nature', and it does this by providing access to an impressive variety of animals, such as giant panda bears in *Amazing Asian Animals*, koala bears and kangaroos in *Aqua City*, where there is also a big aquarium, penguins in *Polar Adventure* and seals in *Marine World*, to name but a few. It has a veterinary centre and a marine mammal breeding and research centre on site and offers a 'Get Closer To The Animals' programme that allows behind the scenes access for an extra fee. Some of the themed lands also include amusement park style attractions and thrill rides, as well as VR attractions and a VR Coaster. More information at www.oceanpark.com.hk (Accessed: 30 August 2018).

Operation Black Antler, Blast Theory and Hydrocracker 2017

Operation Black Antler is an immersive theatre production that explores surveillance. Participants are given a new identity before being sent on an undercover mission in a small group. Participants then have to make a number of decisions that will impact the course of the narrative, and are asked to reflect on the ethics of those decisions. More information at www.blasttheory.co.uk/projects/operation-black-antler/ (Accessed: 22 August 2018).

Pokémon Go, Niantic and Nintendo 2016

Pokémon Go is an augmented reality game for iOS and Android. Free to download, the game has proved to be immensely popular internationally (more than 800 million downloads), and has been the subject of much press attention and scrutiny. In the game, players have an avatar and can see themselves represented on a map based on their real-world geographical location. They can then move through this augmented landscape battling and collecting *Pokémon* as they go. More information at www.pokemongo.com/en-us/ (Accessed: 22 August 2018).

122 *Glossary of Examples*

Project Syria, **Nonny de la Peña 2014**

Project Syria was commissioned by the World Economic Forum as a work of immersive journalism. It uses audio visual resources and a first-person perspective virtual reality experience. Its ambition is to educate people about the plight of child refugees in Syria by 'transport[ing] audiences to the scene as the story unfolds'. More information at https://store.steampowered.com/app/491790/Project_Syria/ (Accessed: 11 May 2018).

Rain Room, **Random International 2012**

Rain Room is an immersive installation in a blackened room where interactants can walk through a downpour of continuous rain, but because of motion sensors installed in the environment, never actually get wet. The experience reflects on the relationship between humans, nature, and technology. More information at www.random-international.com/rain-room-2012 (Accessed: 22 August 2018).

River of Mud, **Tadeu Jungle 2016**

River of Mud (Rio de Lama) is a 360 degree documentary about the Samarco Dam environmental disaster in Brazil, November 2015. The documentary details the impacts of the disaster on the local community. More information at https://docubase.mit.edu/project/river-of-mud/ (Accessed: 18 June 2018).

Secret Cinema

Since 2007, *Secret Cinema* have been staging immersive cinema experiences 'where the boundaries between performer and audience, set and reality are constantly shifting'. Participants in the storyworlds created are often unaware of what awaits them as the experiences are shrouded in mystery. The *Secret Cinema* website features video highlights of past productions. More information at www.secretcinema.org/ (Accessed: 22 August 2018).

Small Wonders, **Punchdrunk, LIFT and Bernie Grant Arts Centre 2018**

Small Wonders was an immersive theatre production for children. Starting on the set of a flat in Tottenham, London, Nanny Lacey vividly recounted her life's adventures through the telling of stories in interaction with her granddaughter Bella and through the use of miniatures. The children were then invited to become immersed in one of Nanny Lacey's miniatures, accompanying them on one last adventure. More information at www.punchdrunk.org.uk/small-wonders/ (Accessed: 4 September 2018).

Somnai, dotdotdot 2018

This blended immersive theatre and virtual reality experience was designed to explore lucid dreaming at what is set up as a sleep clinic, but is actually a converted warehouse in London. Six participants at a time are given pyjamas and introduced to a dream guide who initiates them into their experience. *Somnai* was a layered and multisensual mixed reality experience. More information at www.dotdot.london/ (Accessed: 18 June 2018).

Tiltbrush

Tiltbrush enables you to paint in 3D in VR via the Oculus Rift and HTC Vive, and to share your creations. More information at www.tiltbrush.com/ (Accessed: 22 August 2018).

Traces/Olion, yello brick, Amgueddfa Cymru National Museum Wales and Cardiff University 2016

Traces (*Olion* in the Welsh language) is a site-specific mobile storytelling application for use at St Fagans National Museum of History, part of Amgueddfa Cymru, National Museum Wales. It is available free to download via iOS and Android, and users can opt for either the single person encounter or the two-person experience where both participants are sent on different – but intersecting – journeys. More information in Chapter 3 of this book and in Huws et al. (2019).

'Under', Martina Amati

This immersive installation uses audiovisual resources to explore the challenging – yet serene – underwater world of freediving. 'Under' has been presented in a number of different ways, but each is conceived to offer interactants a vivid experience of what it is like to be under the water without breathing equipment. 'Under' was funded by a Wellcome Arts Award. More information at https://wellcomecollection.org/installations/Wrynhx8AAAjk9XX- (Accessed: 22 August 2018).

VAN Beethoven, LA Philharmonic Orchestra 2015

VAN Beethoven was a virtual reality experience featuring the LA Philharmonic Orchestra (headed by its star conductor Gustavo Dudamel) playing the opening four minutes of Beethoven's *Symphony No. 5 in C Minor*, accompanied by a series of animations swirling in the air around the performers themselves. The experience was accessed in a purpose-built mobile theatre fitted with Oculus headsets.

With New Eyes I See, yello brick, Amgueddfa Cymru National Museum Wales and Cardiff University 2013

With New Eyes I See (WNEIS) was a prototype site-specific digital heritage encounter that transformed the civic centre of Cardiff, as archival materials were physically projected onto, and playfully manipulated by, buildings and the natural environment. Audiences had to piece together a narrative from projections on walls and monuments, animations, found objects, documents, a soundscape, and the voice of an unidentified narrator. *WNEIS* was an experiment in taking narrative beyond the screen or the interpretation panel, working with archival materials to tell stories beyond the walls of the museum. More information in Kidd (2017).

Glossary of Examples 125

Harry Potter Storyworld

This is not a complete list of genres that can be found within the *Harry Potter* storyworld, but rather only of the examples we have referred to in this book. It is also not a summary of content. As there is some repetition of names across genres, we have listed examples by name and then briefly summarised the different forms this name appears as.

Diagon Alley (themed land)

Diagon Alley is a themed land created by Universal as part of their Universal Studios Florida theme park in Orlando, Florida. It was opened in 2014 and includes a section of 'muggle' (i.e. non-magical) London with Kings Cross station (where the '**Hogwarts Express**' attraction links this themed land with *Hogsmeade* at Universal Islands of Adventure), as well as the wizarding shopping areas of Diagon Alley, Horizon Alley, Knockturn Alley, and Carkitt Market. It includes the ride '**Harry Potter and the Escape from Gringotts**', as well as Harry Potter themed retail and food and drink outlets, including Ollivander's wand shop where visitors can see/take part in a wand selection experience). Interactive wands are available with which visitors can cast spells at certain locations in the themed lands.

Fantastic Beasts and Where to Find Them (fictitious textbook, feature film)

Fantastic Beasts and Where to Find Them by J.K. Rowling. This book was initially mentioned in the *Harry Potter* books as a textbook and was released in aid of charity Comic Relief in 2011 with J.K. Rowling writing and illustrating as Newt Scamander. As such it is sometimes referred to as an 'in-universe' book or one of the '**Hogwarts Library Books**'. In 2017, an illustrated (and slightly extended) version was published with illustrations by Olivia Lomenech Gill, which has also been turned into a Kindle in Motion book (which animates the illustrations), released in 2018. *Fantastic Beasts and Where to Find Them* has since also become the title of a feature film, written by J.K. Rowling, directed by David Yates, and released in 2016. The film is not an adaptation of the book, however, but could be considered a prequel to the original **Harry Potter novels** in that it is set in the Wizarding World (albeit in America, rather than the UK, and during an earlier time). Warner

Bros. have announced that this is the first in a five-part series of movies, with the next one, *The Crimes of Grindelwald*, released in November 2018. More information at www.fantasticbeasts.co.uk (Accessed: 1 September 2018).

Flight of the Hippogriff (theme park ride)

'Flight of the Hippogriff' is a short roller coaster ride located in the themed land *Hogsmeade* at Universal Islands of Adventure and Universal Studios Japan. The theming of the queue is outside and passes Hagrid's hut, but the ride itself is not a dark ride and doesn't really tell a story.

Harry Potter: A History of Magic (exhibition and exhibition catalogue)

Harry Potter: A History of Magic was an exhibition curated by the British Library at their PACCAR Gallery in London. It ran from 20 October 2017 to 28 February 2018 (more information at www.bl.uk/events/harry-potter-a-history-of-magic; accessed: 1 September 2018). Planned to coincide with the twentieth anniversary of the publication of *Harry Potter and the Philosopher's Stone*, the artefacts shown included a mixture of things that were from the archive of J.K. Rowling and Bloomsbury, such as sketches and drafts of the writing of the original novels, illustrations by Jim Kay and Olivia Lomenech Gill, as well as artefacts from the British Library's collection (and other museums') that explored the folklore of magic. Scheduled to coincide with the exhibition, there were displays inspired by it in a number of public libraries around Great Britain (more information at www.bl.uk/projects/harry-potter-a-history-of-magic-public-library-displays; accessed: 1 September 2018). The exhibition was transferred to the New York Historical Society Museum & Library, where it was scheduled between 5 October 2018 and 27 January 2019. The New York version also includes some of the artwork from US editions by Brian Selznick and Mary GrandPré, as well as artefacts relating to the Broadway production of *Harry Potter and the Cursed Child* (more information at http://m.nyhistory.org/exhibition/harry-potter-history-magic; accessed: 1 September 2018). Two companion books were published (in 2017 by Bloomsbury in the UK and Scholastic in the US): a traditional catalogue called *Harry Potter: A History of Magic*, and *Harry Potter: A Journey Through a History of Magic*, which is aimed at families and showcases a selection of the artefacts for a younger audience. In October 2018, an audiobook of the catalogue was published, containing 'a host of original interview material curated especially for this production' (Pottermore News Team, 2018).

Harry Potter and the Chamber of Secrets (novel, audiobook, feature film, video game)

Harry Potter and the Chamber of Secrets by J.K. Rowling. Originally published in 1998, this is the second of the novels making up the original seven-book *Harry Potter* series. An unabridged audiobook was released with the voice of Stephen Fry (UK) and Jim Dale (US). In 2002, a feature film based on it was released by Warner Bros., directed by Chris Columbus. A video game was released for multiple platforms in the same year by Electronic Arts. In 2016, an illustrated edition of the novel was released with illustrations by Jim Kay.

Harry Potter and the Cursed Child – Parts 1 and 2 (play)

Harry Potter and the Cursed Child, a play in two parts written by Jack Thorne based on a story by J.K. Rowling, Jack Thorne, and John Tiffany. It is set 19+ years after *Harry Potter and the Deathly Hallows* finishes, with the first scene overlapping the epilogue of that book. The play script for both parts was released in 2016, coinciding with the premiere of the play at the Palace Theatre in London, directed by John Tiffany. A second production was opened in 2018 at the Lyric Theatre in New York, and a forthcoming production has been announced for Melbourne's Princess Theatre 2019.

Harry Potter and the Deathly Hallows (novel, audiobook, feature film, video game)

Harry Potter and the Deathly Hallows by J.K. Rowling. Originally published in 2007, this is the seventh of the novels making up the original seven-book *Harry Potter* series. An unabridged audiobook was released with the voice of Stephen Fry (UK) and Jim Dale (US). When adapting this book into feature film, Warner Bros. made the decision to split it over two, with Part 1 being released in 2010 and Part 2 in 2011. They were both directed by David Yates. Electronic Arts released games for multiple platforms corresponding with both films' release dates.

Harry Potter and the Escape from Gringotts (theme park ride)

'Harry Potter and the Escape from Gringotts' is a dark ride located in Gringotts Wizarding Bank in the ***Diagon Alley*** themed land. The queue explores the bank, first entrance hall, and then its vaults where visitors get their picture taken for a security check as they are there to open an account (and later can purchase their bank ID with their photograph). Carts take riders on the ride to deliver the story, using motion and 3D projections. Not all actors returned to record dialogue for this attraction. It opened in 2014.

Harry Potter and the Forbidden Journey (theme park ride)

'Harry Potter and the Forbidden Journey' is a dark ride located in Hogwarts Castle in the ***Hogsmeade*** themed lands. The queue snakes through the castle, taking in the dungeons, green houses, classrooms, etc. The ride vehicles are 'enchanted' benches and the ride uses motion and projection to deliver the story. Filmed sections include characters from the movies, played by the same actors as in the movies. The original ride was opened in 2010 at Islands of Adventures.

Harry Potter and the Goblet of Fire (novel, audiobook, feature film, video game)

Harry Potter and the Goblet of Fire by J.K. Rowling. Originally published in 2000, this is the fourth of the novels making up the original seven-book *Harry Potter* series. An unabridged audiobook was released with the voice of Stephen Fry (UK) and Jim Dale (US). In 2005, a feature film based on it was released by Warner Bros., directed by Mike Newell. The same year a corresponding video game was released for multiple platforms by Electronic Arts. Illustrator Jim Kay is currently working on an illustrated edition of this book, to be released in 2019.

Harry Potter and the Half-Blood Prince (novel, audiobook, feature film, video game)

Harry Potter and the Half-Blood Prince by J.K. Rowling. Originally published in 2005, this is the sixth of the novels making up the original seven-book *Harry Potter* series. An unabridged audiobook was released with the voice of Stephen Fry (UK) and Jim Dale (US). In 2009, a feature film based on it was released by Warner Bros., directed by David Yates. The same year a video game was released for multiple platforms by Electronic Arts.

Harry Potter and the Order of the Phoenix (novel, audiobook, feature film, video game)

Harry Potter and the Order of the Phoenix by J.K. Rowling. Originally published in 2003, this is the fifth of the novels making up the original seven-book *Harry Potter* series. An unabridged audiobook was released with the voice of Stephen Fry (UK) and Jim Dale (US). In 2007, a feature film based on it was released by Warner Bros., directed by David Yates. The same year a corresponding video game was released for multiple platforms.

Harry Potter and the Philosopher's Stone (novel, audiobook, feature film, video game)

Harry Potter and the Philosopher's Stone by J.K. Rowling. Originally published in 1997, this is the first of the novels making up the original seven-book *Harry Potter* series. In the US, it was published under the name *Harry Potter and the Sorcerer's Stone*. An unabridged audiobook was released with the voice of Stephen Fry (UK) and Jim Dale (US). In 2001, a feature film based on it was released by Warner Bros., directed by Chris Columbus (again titled *Harry Potter and the Sorcerer's Stone* in the US). Video games were developed for five consoles to be released at the same time as the film by Electronic Arts. In 2015, an illustrated edition of the novel was released with illustrations by Jim Kay.

Harry Potter and the Prisoner of Azkaban (novel, audiobook, feature film, video game)

Harry Potter and the Prisoner of Azkaban by J.K. Rowling. Originally published in 1999, this is the third of the novels making up the original seven-book *Harry Potter* series. An unabridged audiobook was released with the voice of Stephen Fry (UK) and Jim Dale (US). In 2004, a feature film based on it was released by Warner Bros., directed by Alfonso Cuarón. The same year saw a release of a corresponding trio of video games for different platforms, the Game Boy Advance one being markedly different as it was a Role Playing Game. In 2017, an illustrated edition of the novel was released with illustrations by Jim Kay.

Harry Potter novels

The original seven Harry Potter novels by J.K. Rowling are at the core of this canon. In order of their publication, they were: ***Harry Potter and the Philosopher's Stone*** (named *Harry Potter and the Sorcerer's Stone* in the US), ***Harry Potter and the Chamber of Secrets***, ***Harry Potter and the Prisoner of Azkaban***, ***Harry Potter and the Goblet of Fire***, ***Harry Potter and the Order of the Phoenix***, ***Harry Potter and the Half-Blood Prince***, and ***Harry Potter and the Deathly Hallows***. For details of their publication date and the genres into which they have been adapted, see their individual entries in this Glossary.

Hogsmeade (themed land)

Hogsmeade (sometimes referred to as *Hogsmeade Village*) is a themed land originally created by Universal as part of their Islands of Adventure theme park in Orlando, Florida. It opened in 2010 and includes a recreation of Hogwarts Castle and the village of Hogsmeade. It includes the rides '**Harry Potter and the Forbidden Journey**' and '**Flight of the Hippogriff**'. The 'Dragon Challenge' ride that was included when it opened is currently closed and will be replaced by a new attraction. As part of Hogsmeade village, there are a number of retail outlets (including another outlet of Ollivander's wand shop in which visitors can see/take part in a wand selection experience) and food and drink places, which are all *Harry Potter* themed. In 2014, Hogsmeade station was opened with the '**Hogwarts Express**', a ride that connects this themed land to **Diagon Alley**, which is located within the Universal Studios Florida theme park. A *Hogsmeade* themed land has also opened at Universal Studios Japan (2014) and Universal Studios Hollywood (2016). These two are slightly different, neither including the '**Hogwarts Express**', and the Hollywood one does not include the '**Flight of the Hippogriff**' either. Japan instead includes a Black Lake and live owls. Interactive wands are available with which visitors can cast spells at certain locations in the themed lands.

Hogwarts Express (theme park ride)

'Hogwarts Express' is an attraction simulating a train ride. It is also a people mover that takes visitors with a Park-to-Park ticket from **Diagon Alley** at Universal Studios Florida to **Hogsmeade** at Universal Islands of Adventure and back. Riders sit within train carriages and projections on both sides convey the story (at the aisle side with overheard conversations and silhouettes of characters, and through seeing what is going on outside 'through' the window). The experience differs depending on which direction you ride. Not all actors from the films were reprising their roles for this. It was opened in 2014.

Hogwarts Library Books

'Hogwarts Library Books' is the combined name of the 'in-universe' books *Fantastic Beasts and Where to Find Them*, *Quidditch Through the Ages* and *The Tales of Beedle the Bard*. They were all short books written by J.K. Rowling in aid of charity and inspired by book titles mentioned in the original seven ***Harry Potter* novels**.

Lego Harry Potter **(play sets, video games)**

Lego Harry Potter refers to sets of Lego that model characters and scenes from the books and films. The first of these sets were released in 2001 coinciding with the release of the ***Harry Potter and the Philosopher's Stone*** feature film. *Lego Harry Potter: Years 1–4* and *Lego Harry Potter: Years 5–7* are two Lego themed video games published by Warner Bros. in 2010 and 2011, respectively. The first one draws on action from the first four novels and films, and the second one from the last three novels (and last four films).

The Making of Harry Potter **(exhibition)**

The Making of Harry Potter (officially *Warner Bros. Studio Tour London – The Making of Harry Potter*) is located in two soundstages adjacent to the working film studios in Leavesden, UK, where all eight Harry Potter feature films were in production. It showcases a number of original sets, costumes and props from the making of the movies, as well as some white card models of some of the built locations and a scale model of the castle. There are also behind the scenes looks at how the special and visual effects in the films were created. Occasionally there are special exhibitions such as showcasing props and costume from a specific movie for a few months or dressing the sets for a season. It was opened in 2012. More information can be found at: www.wbstudiotour.co.uk/ (Accessed: 1 September 2018).

Pottermore **(website)**

Pottermore is a website exploring 'the digital heart of the wizarding world'. It was initially published in 2012, and is a collection of news, features, and articles collecting and commenting on the Wizarding World created by J.K. Rowling. It also publishes short new writings by Rowling that extend the *Harry Potter* storyworld by providing more details. It is available at: www.pottermore.com (Accessed: 1 September 2018).

The Wizarding World of Harry Potter (themed lands)

The Wizarding World of Harry Potter is the term describing the *Harry Potter* themed lands that have been created by Universal as part of their theme parks. Currently, there are two different ones: ***Hogsmeade*** and ***Diagon Alley***. It should be noted that *The Wizarding World of Harry Potter* at the Universal Orlando Resort is not an independent theme park, but rather two themed lands in two different theme parks – ***Hogsmeade*** at Universal's Islands of Adventure and ***Diagon Alley*** at Universal Studios Florida. They are linked by the '**Hogwarts Express**' ride, for which a Park-to-Park admission ticket is required. At the other Universal parks (Hollywood and Japan), only one of the themed lands (***Hogsmeade***) currently exists.

Index

absorption 22, 58n1, 92
Amgueddfa Cymru - National Museum Wales (ACNMW) 66, 123–124
adaptation 20n2, 21–22, 54, 59, 119
adaptive characteristics 49, 53–57
addiction 94–97
aesthetic capitalism 19, 85, 93, 100
affordances (of genre) 18, 22–23, 26
agency 19, 85, 95; complicated 88–89, 93, 100–101, 102, 106; participants' 27, 29–31, 33, 39, 47, 55, 77, 82
alternate reality gaming 91
analogy 2–5, 90, 105
appropriation 91
app (Applications) 10–11, 13, 40, 62–63, 66–68, *69*, *71*, 74, 76, 78, 81, 118, 120, 123
audience 9–10, 13–17, 21, 24, 26–27, 29–31, 33, 41, 47, 58n5, 62, 67–68, 85–86, 89–92, 94, 101
audiobook 26–27, 39, 42, 48, 74, 126–128
Augmented Reality (AR) 1, 10–12, 40, 87, 97, 101, 117, 121
Augmented Reality Immersive Team Trainer 11, 117

backstory 2–3, 49–51
Blade Runner (*Secret Cinema*) 92
Bordergame 86, 117–118
bounded experience 23
Breathe 9, 20n4, 118
buy-in 56, 94

Cambridge Analytica 88
capitalism 99–100; aesthetic 19, 85, 93, 100; surveillance 99
characters 3, 6–7, 31, 49–50, 53–54, 58n3, 64–65, 81, 94
Choose Your Own Ending/ Adventure books 9
cognition 17, 117
commodity fetishism 96
complicated agency 88–89, 93, 100–101, 102, 106
computer games 9
consistency 53–54, 59n8; sensory 47–48, 59
consumer(s) 30; culture 85; passive 30; spaces 22
consumption 14, 29, 32–33, 91–93, 103n3
CosPlay 7, 17, 58n5
creation 8, 17, 22, 27, *28*, 28, 33, 36, 37–48, 58, 59n10, 60, 61–65, 81, 83, 87, 105
creative industries 93, 103n2
creator 23, 27, 33–37, 58n5, 62
critiques of immersion 85–103
cultural capital 90

democratisation 88, 93
Diagon Alley 32, 35, 40, 42–43, *44*, 47–48, 124, 128, 130–132
digitality 86
disempower 89, 100
distribution 14
divers 3

economy: experience 19, 22, 85, 91–92, 94; sharing 88
embodied 17–18, 105
empowerment 90
engagement 11, 33, 42, 79, 83, 85, 94–97
English (Fiona) 22–28, 42
escapism 58(n), 81, 85, 94, 96, 101
ethics 19, 117, 121
exhibition 34, 36–39, 41, *41*, 48, 50–52, 54, 59n7, 125–126, 131
experience(s): audio 26; bounded 23; economy 19, 22, 85, 91–92, 94; industry 91; kinaesthetic 24, 35, 56, 63; mixed reality 123; sensory 105; visceral 24
experiential marketing 22, 93
exploitation 87, 100
Extended Reality (XR) 10, 12, 87
Extinct 86, 101, 118

Facebook 9, 88, 98, 100
fans 15, 48, 58n5, 96
Fantastic Beasts and Where to Find Them: book 125, 131; film(s) 50, 125
field notes 62, *62*
film 7, 9, 20n2, 24–25, 35, 38–40, 48–50, 52–54, 56, 58n5, 92, 94–95, 118–119, 125–129
flow 11
fourth wall 14
frame-breaking 87
framework: Layers of Experience framework 18, 21–60, 84, 104–106; Orientations of Genres framework 22–23, 27–28
framing 14, 24, 26, 51, 72, 74–75, 87, 89
franchise 15, 17–18, 23, 36, 60, 100

gains and losses 22
games: computer 9; street 1, 15, 67
gaming disorder 94
genre 1, 7, 18, 21–29, 33–36, 38–39, 47–50, 52–56, 66, 70, 95–97, 105
See also Orientations of Genres Framework

glass-bottomed boat of research (also see analogy) 2–5, 105
guest(s) 3, 15, 27, 29–31, 43, 49, 102

haptic 7, 11, 13, 78, 120
Harry Potter: A History of Magic 34, 37–39, 41, *41*, 48, 50, 52, 54, 56, 125–126; **and the Cursed Child** 25, 32, 34, 53, 126–127; **and the Escape from Gringotts** 35, 42, 47, 127; **and the Forbidden Journey** 31, 128; ***and the Philosopher's Stone\ and the Sorcerer's Stone*** 52, 128–129; ***and the Prisoner of Azkaban*** 56, 129; British Library exhibition (see *Harry Potter: A History of Magic*); films 24; *Fantastic Beasts and Where to Find Them* 50, 125, 131; *Lego Harry Potter* 52, 131; *The Making of Harry Potter* 35–36, 38, 40, 46, 48, 54, 56, 131; merchandise 25, 32, 46; **novels** 30, 32, 35, 38, 42, 50, 52–53, 130; play (see *Harry Potter and the Cursed Child*); *Pottermore* 50, 59n9, 132; studio tour (see *The Making of Harry Potter*); storyworld 17–18, 23–25, 29, 36, 39, 46, 51, 54–55, 94, 105, 125–131; themed lands (see *The Wizarding World of Harry Potter*, *Diagon Alley* and *Hogsmeade*); *The Wizarding World of Harry Potter* 31–32, 40, *44*, 46, 56, *57*, 131
hippogriff 24, 125
Hogsmeade 40, 42, 45, 56, *57*, 130–132
Hogwarts Express 42, 47, 130
Hold The World 101, 118
Hunger in Los Angeles 86, 118
hypertext 9, 54, 89
hypotext 54

I Am A Man 86, 119
identity 8, 26–27, 33, 36–37, 70
immersion: conceptual 17, 82; sensual 17; phenomenological 17
immersive: art applications 11; book 6; documentaries 11;

Index   135

fiction reading 12; journalism 11, 20, 86, 106, 122; music 11; theatre 1, 2, 5, 13–15, 21, 67, 86–87, 89–91, 106, 117, 120–123
interactant(s) 30, 89
interactive wands 31, 45, 47, 125, 130
It's No Game 11, 119

Jekyll 2.0 11, 119–120

Kay (Jim) 38, 48, 126–129
kinaesthetic 24, 35, 42, 47, 56, 63

Lanark 9
Last Action Hero, The 7
Letter, The 101, 120
linearity 28, 49, 51, 82
liquid immersion/metaphor 4–5, 90, 104, 106
Live Action Role Playing (LARPing) 7, 17
Lost in Austen 7
Lost Palace, The 13, 101, 120

Making of Harry Potter, The (studio tour) 35–36, 38, 40, 46, 48, 54, 56, 131
Masque of the Red Death, The 90, 120
Mercedes - AMG GT launch 94
merchandise 25, 32, 46, 96
metaphor 5, 104, 106
mode(s): auditory 42–43, 96; gustatory 24, 46; kinaesthetic 24, 42, 47, 56, 63; olfactory 46, 56; tactile 45–46, 56, 79; visual 17, 24, 26, 40–43, 54, 56, 96
motivation 31–35, 66
Museum View 88

narrative: branching and foldback 68; linearity 9–10, 28, 49, 51, 65, 81–82; two person 61, 63–70, 77–78
neoliberalism 91, 100–101
Neverending Story, The 6–7, 20n2 n3
novel 6–7, 9, 24–26, 32, 35, 36, 38, 48–55

Ocean Park *16*, 101, 121
Olion (see *Traces/Olion*)
Operation Black Antler 86, 121

orientations: creation 17, 22, 27–28, 37–48, 58, 60–65, 83, 105; participant 17, 19, 22, 27–28, 29–33, 60–61, 70–81; process 17, 19, 22, 27–28, 33–37, 48, 60, 66–70, 84, 105; story 17, 19, 22, 27–28, 48–58, 61, 68, 81–84, 105–106
Orientations of Genres framework 22, 23, 28
ownership 36–37

participant(s) 5, 10, 14, 16, 17, 19, 22, 27–33, 39, 43, 45, 47–48, 50–51, 54–56, 58, 61, 63–65, 68, 70–81, 82, 84, 89, 92, 94, 100–102, 105–106, 117–123
participation: entrepreneurial 90; paradigm 88
participatory culture 88, 99
performance society 93
player(s) 30, 40, 52–53, 95–96
playscript 25, 34
plot 35, 38, 49, 51–52, 54
Pokémon Go 12, 101, 121
Pottermore 50, 59
power 1, 8, 19, 30, 85–90, 96, 99–101, 106
presence 10–11, 83, 94, 97
Project Syria 101, 122
Purple Rose of Cairo, The 7
Punchdrunk 14, 90, 120, 122–123

Rain Room 11, *12*, 122
reader(s) 6–7, 9, 26, 30, 50, 52–53, 56, 58, 90
regenreing 22–23
remediation 21
role 27, 29–31, 33, 36–37, 53, 55, 63, 67, 70, 78
Rowling (J.K.) 23, 34–36, 38, 46, 50, 52, 125–132
ride (theme park) 3, 24, 31–33 35–36, 42, 47, 55
rider(s) 24, 30, 33
River of Mud 11, 122
roller coaster 24, 33, 47, 126

S 9
Secret Cinema 91–92, 122

senses: proprioception 24, 47, 56; sight 24, 42–43, 54, 56; smell 6, 24, 46–47, 56, 65, 70, 78–79; sound 25, 43, 45, 47, 54, 56, 76, 78, 120, 124; taste 6, 24, 46–47, 56; touch 24, 45–46, 56, 63, 65–66, 68, 78
sensory consistency 47–48, 59
site: -flexible 32, 39; -generic 39; -specific/designed 13, 39–40, 64
Small Wonders 14, 130–131
social justice 19, 86, 97
Somnai 86, 123
spaces: consumer 22, 91, 100, 106; entertainment 22, 91; virtual 22, 38, 40, 83
spectatorship 13, 15, 89, 92
stereoscopic (3D) technology 24
St Fagans National Museum of History, Wales 13, 60, 63–84, 123
storytelling: history of 2, 8–14; interactive 10, 68, 85, 87, 93, 100, 119; web 9, 13, 89
storyworlds: franchise 15, 17–18, 23, 100; transmedia 15, 22, 83, 91, 101, 106
street games/gaming 1, 15, 21, 67–68, 106, 118
surveillance: capitalism 99; realism 99
suspension of disbelief 55
swimmers 3

technocratic 86, 97
technoliberalism 99
text 7, 13, 25–26, 35–36
theatre, see immersive theatre
themed lands 18, 20, 23, 25, 31, 32, 35–36, 40, 43–46, 48, 56, 101, 121, 125–126, 128, 130–132
theme park 1–3, 5, 12, 15, 18, 20, 22, 24, 32, 36, 40, 45, 47–49, 55, 90, 95–96, 121, 124–125, 127, 129–130, 131; ride 3, 24, 31–33, 35–36, 42, 47, 55, 121, 124–125, 128–132
Thursday Next 7
time 37, 45, 63
Tiltbrush 11, 123

topics and themes 25, 38, 63, 73
Traces/Olion 13, 14, 18–19, 60–84, *61*, *71*, *73*, *78*, 105–106, 123
transmedia 1, 15, 17, 21–22, 83, 91, 101, 106
triangulation 61, 82, 105
tyranny 9, 89

Under 5–6, *6*, 123
Unfortunates, The 9
Universal: Creative 35; Islands of Adventure 40, 57, 124, 125, 127, 129–131; Studios, Florida 32, 35, 40, 42–43, 124, 130–131; Studios, Hollywood 40, 130–131; Studios, Japan 40, 126, 130–132

value chain of cultural consumption 14, 34
videogame(s) 3, 10, 11, 24–25, 39–40, 47, 52, 55, 94–96, 126–129, 131
Virtual Reality (VR) 1, 22, 86, 106, 118, 122–124
virtual space 22, 38, 40, 83
visitor(s) 12, 29–31, 35, 40, 41–43, 46–47, 49, 52, 56, 67–68, 79–80, 82, 90, 125, 128, 130

waders 3
wands, interactive 31, 45, 47, 125, 130
water analogy 2–5, 90
Welsh language 60, 63, 67–68, 78, 123
With New Eyes I See 66, 124
Wizarding World of Harry Potter, The 18, 31–32, 40, 44, 46, 56–57, 131; *Diagon Alley* 32, 35, 40, 42–43, *44*, 47–48, 124, 127, 130–131; *Hogsmeade* 40, 42, 45, 56–57, *57*, 124, 125, 128, 130–132
World of Warcraft 9
World Wide Web 9, 98

XR (see Extended Reality)

yello brick 61, 66–68, 86, 118, 123–124
YouTube 9, 14, 87, 94, 98, 100

For Product Safety Concerns and Information please contact our EU
representative GPSR@taylorandfrancis.com
Taylor & Francis Verlag GmbH, Kaufingerstraße 24, 80331 München, Germany

www.ingramcontent.com/pod-product-compliance
Lightning Source LLC
Chambersburg PA
CBHW070738230426
43669CB00014B/2495